❖ Injustice ❖
FOR All

"Priscilla H. Machado Zotti has done for Dollree Mapp what Anthony Lewis in *Gideon's Trumpet* did for Clarence Gideon. A riveting tale, well told, of a landmark Supreme Court decision that will engage legal scholars and all interested in the law."
David O'Brien, Leone Reaves and George W. Spicer Professor,
University of Virginia, Charlottesville, Virginia

"A riveting account of the drama behind one of the U.S. Supreme Court's most celebrated landmarks in criminal justice. Readers will discover a compelling cast of characters from the earnest cop to the streetwise moll to the contentious justices of the historic Warren Court—all brought to life by Zotti's painstaking research and colorful descriptions."
Barbara Perry, Carter Glass Professor and Chair,
Sweet Briar College, Sweet Briar, Virginia

➤ Injustice ➤

FOR All

TEACHING TEXTS IN LAW AND POLITICS

David A. Schultz
General Editor

Vol. 39

PETER LANG
New York • Washington, D.C./Baltimore • Bern
Frankfurt am Main • Berlin • Brussels • Vienna • Oxford

Priscilla H. Machado Zotti

⇒•Injustice•⇐
FOR All

Mapp vs. Ohio

and the

Fourth Amendment

PETER LANG
New York • Washington, D.C./Baltimore • Bern
Frankfurt am Main • Berlin • Brussels • Vienna • Oxford

Library of Congress Cataloging-in-Publication Data

Zotti, Priscilla Machado.
Injustice for all: Mapp vs. Ohio and the Fourth Amendment /
Priscilla H. Machado Zotti.
p. cm. — (Teaching texts in law and politics; v. 39)
Includes bibliographical references and index.
1. Mapp, Dollree—Trials, litigation, etc.
2. Exclusionary rule (Evidence)—United States.
I. Title. II. Series.
KF224.M213Z68   345.73'0522—dc22   2004011678
ISBN 0-8204-7267-0
ISSN 1083-3447

Bibliographic information published by **Die Deutsche Bibliothek**.
Die Deutsche Bibliothek lists this publication in the "Deutsche
Nationalbibliografie"; detailed bibliographic data is available
on the Internet at http://dnb.ddb.de/.

Cover design by Lisa Barfield

For Steve

✤ TABLE OF CONTENTS

✤ ILLUSTRATIONS

✢ PREFACE

I have been interested in the Fourth Amendment for all of my professional life. Encapsulated in its clauses is the ultimate test of a democracy; how it's citizens are treated by agents of the government in situations when the individual is vulnerable. The requirement of reasonableness is vague. How courts interpret a blunt legal instrument to satisfy both individual liberty and public safety underscores the tension of the Constitution, and in our society, between those who abide by the law and those who break it.

I began looking at the Fourth Amendment historically. Its roots are a fascinating read. The judicial manifestations of both the right and remedy are voluminous and circuitous. In addition to a historical schooling, I have studied search and seizure rights abroad and from a comparative perspective. As public policy and as a backdrop to understanding judicial behavior, the Fourth Amendment is rich. The book I have written is a culmination of all of these approaches with the addition of the most important—a human story. When I first began researching the case of Dollree Mapp, it was the human element that drew me in. The most prominent figures involved in the case seemed larger than life. Carl Delau, Michael Haney, Donald King, the justices of the Supreme Court and of course, Dollree Mapp herself, together weave a tale that addresses all the interests I have in the Fourth Amendment. I have tried to tell their story and, through it, tell the larger story of a constitutional right and its role in a free society.

How difficult it must be to serve as a police officer. How purposeful one must be to challenge the status quo all the way to the Supreme Court of the United States. The original documents taught me a great deal. Reading newspapers from the 1960s, studying old trial transcripts, and staring at photographs of a beautiful black woman and an eager and honest police officer, gained me perspective. I think the book is richer as a result of time, meticulous research, and a deep appreciation of the history, political, and social aspects to this constitutional provision.

As I was writing late one afternoon, I received a package in the mail. It was from Carl Delau, the police officer who conducted the search of Dollree Mapp's home. On the face of the brown envelope it read "Priscilla—Why wait any longer—This is now all yours. Perhaps, a piece of history. Carl." Inside was the now yellow-aged paper at the heart of the controversy of *Mapp v. Ohio*. This is a great story. I hope I tell it well.

Priscilla H. M. Zotti, Ph.D.
United States Naval Academy
Annapolis, Maryland

✢ ACKNOWLEDGMENTS

Many of the source materials used in the writing of this book are original documents and personal interviews. My goal was an authentic and clear reading of the case of *Mapp v. Ohio* and the surrounding information. Below is a list of documentary sources and persons interviewed. If I have failed to mention any source, it is an inadvertent omission.

Library of Congress, Manuscript Room, Washington, D.C.
    Papers of Hugo Black
    Papers of William Brennan
    Papers of Warren Burger
    Papers of William O. Douglas
    Papers of Felix Frankfurter
    Papers of John Marshall Harlan
    Papers of Robert Jackson
    Papers of Thurgood Marshall
    Papers of Earl Warren
    Papers of Byron White
    Papers of Charles Whittaker

Library of Congress, Periodical Room, Washington, D.C.
    Village Voice
    New York Times
    Cleveland News
    Cleveland Plain Dealer

Supreme Court of the United States, Washington, D.C.
    Library
    Office of the Clerk

Harvard Law School, Manuscript Collection, Boston, Massachusetts
    Papers of Felix Frankfurter

Tarlton Law Library, The University of Texas at Austin, Special Collections
and Rare Book Room
    Papers of Tom C. Clark

Seeley G. Mudd Manuscript Library, Princeton University, Princeton, New
Jersey
    Papers of the American Civil Liberties Union

Cleveland Public Library, Cleveland, Ohio
    Call and Post
    Cleveland Press
    Cleveland Plain Dealer
    Cleveland Magazine
    Photographic Collection

Howard University, Washington, D.C.
    Call and Post

City of Cleveland Public Records
Cleveland Police Department
Cuyahoga County Public Library
Case Western Reserve Library

Interviews with:

Scott Brantley, Cleveland Office of the Federal Bureau of Investigation
Judge Michael Corrigan, Jr.
Carl Delau
Christopher Evans, *Cleveland Magazine*
Michael Haney
Donald Lybarber
Dollree Mapp
Dorris O'Donnell
E. Barrett Prettyman
Jim Willis

In writing this book there are many individuals I wish to thank for their support. Some of these individuals I know through my professional life; others are dear friends and family. All contributed to the final outcome of this work through their support and assistance. Any errors are mine alone.

At the United States Naval Academy, I have received support from various parts of the institution. The Naval Academy Research Council assisted in summer research funding. The Research Office and the Faculty Enhancement Center assisted in travel funds to visit research sites away from the Washington metropolitan area. Linda Hull of the Political Science Department was very helpful with the mechanical aspects of publishing this work. Barbara Breeden of the Naval Academy Library, provided me endless amounts of assistance in finding resource material, some of it from the 1950s. Emily Arnold provided me technical support which was instrumental to the final product. Her expertise was indispensable. Ken Mierzejewski and Shannon O'Connor assisted me with the cover art of the book and the formatting of photos. Thank you all for your contributions.

Professionally, a number of colleagues at other institutions were helpful in reading drafts of the book, even in its earliest stage. Terry Sullivan of the

University of North Carolina at Chapel Hill supported the idea of this book from its infancy. Mary Beeman of the College of Incarnate Word read numerous drafts and spent many an hour discussing with me, her area of expertise, Justice Tom Clark. Mary recently passed away from cancer, but her spirit is alive in the opinion writing portion of this book. Michael Mansfield of Baylor University, who long ago directed my Masters thesis, is a dear friend who has supported me throughout this journey. John Domino of Sam Houston State University, Paul Kens of Southwest Texas State University, Bob Clinton of University of Illinois at Carbondale, David O'Brien of the University of Virginia, and Barbara Perry of Sweetbriar College are all friends and colleagues whose input proved valuable in shaping this book.

Working with the professionals at Peter Lang has been a rewarding experience. Phyllis Korper and Bernadette Shade both were supportive and helpful at every turn. Their attention to detail and prompt replies to my queries made for a smooth working relationship. I thank you both. David Schultz, the series editor, has been equally supportive.

Certain friends went far and beyond to assist me in writing this book. From proofreading to editing, to even watching my children for me while I tackled some collection in a library, friends like Sheila Palmer, Celeste Blessin, and Trinity Menard made life a bit easier for me. Thank you to each of you for your support.

Finally, there is my family. My parents and siblings have always been supporters of my interests. They might not be able to tell you much about the Fourth Amendment, but they all appreciate that it is a topic that fascinates me.

Those individuals who most felt the impact of the writing of this book are my daughters and husband. Caroline, Katherine and Kendall all tolerated my absence and my hours of isolated writing with understanding and support. Each brings me daily joy, a boundless gift, which I cherish.

No one sacrificed more for me than my husband, Steve. He probably knows more about the law of search and seizure than any non-lawyer, non-political scientist should. His support was vital to the completion of this book. Always my biggest fan, I hope I can honor him in some small way by dedicating this work to him.

Priscilla H. M. Zotti
Annapolis, Maryland

CHAPTER ONE
The Bombing

There are several ways to run numbers, and Sergeant Carl I. Delau knew them all. The most common involved bettors choosing a three-digit number from 000 to 999. A particular stock number from stock and bond sales figures in the *Cleveland News* was selected to determine the winner. Since 1954, wagerers could also bet on a number between 1 and 78, and the winner was decided by pulling numbered balls out of a bag. Both games of chance were popular in Cleveland, Ohio, in the 1950s.

Assigned to the powerful Bureau of Special Investigation, Sergeant Delau was acquainted with Cleveland's vice activities. Horse racing and baseball belonged to the whites. Blacks controlled policy and gambling, although this was changing. Pornography was not a large problem, at least not yet. In May of 1957 Delau focused his attention on policy, or numbers wagering. The activities were located primarily in the Sixth and Eighth districts of Cleveland, and Delau was familiar with the principal players. Policy, or clearinghouse, was becoming big business in Cleveland. An illegal game of chance, policy appealed to those of all economic means. Even those with more modest resources could place a wager regularly. They did so often, so much so that the police department of the city of Cleveland formed the Bureau of Special Investigation headed by Lieutenant Martin Cooney, Sergeant Delau's direct superior. The importance of the bureau could not be overstated. Cooney reported directly to the chief of police, Frank W. Story. Delau's chain of command indicated the importance the Cleveland Police Department placed on curtailing vice activities: Delau to Cooney to the chief. The chief of police was very determined to keep Cleveland from being a haven for criminals. He gave Cooney and his Bureau of Special Investigation citywide jurisdiction.

About 3:00 A.M. on May 20, 1957, Sergeant Delau received a telephone call from a resident in the Sixth district. He recognized the voice of twenty-five-year-old Donald King, a young but well-known clearinghouse operator who would later become nationally known as the boxing promoter with "that hair." King sounded desperate and bewildered. "Sergeant, they bombed my house."

"Donald, are you sure?" Delau asked King.

King replied, "I don't have a front porch. I can look out and it's gone. I don't have a front door."

Delau knew that King lived on East 151st Street, not far from the Mount Pleasant Police Station. "Did you call the police?"

"No," King said, "I called you first. You are the only one I can trust." He may have called Delau first, but he had a suspicion who bombed his home. King placed a number of calls to others involved in clearinghouse and policy—others that he suspected were involved. He told them he was not scared and would talk to the police.

Within minutes Delau called in the report and was told to go to King's residence at 3713 E. 151st Street to investigate. There he found a clearly rattled Don King amid the rubble that comprised the street-side portion of his home. By daybreak, fifteen officers were on-site. King's residence, what was left of it, was a crime scene. What happened appeared to be a turf war for control of the policy business in Cleveland. Someone using "muscle" was sending King a powerful message, likely another clearinghouse operator competing with King for business and power. Little did Carl Delau know, this was to begin the long chain of events that would forever change the way police conduct investigations in the United States.

~~~

Cleveland, with a population of 914,808, was a large Midwestern city in 1957. Nestled on the banks of the Cuyahoga River, the city was picturesque and pleasant. It was American dream-houses with garages and white picket fences, safe neighborhoods, good schools, and enclaves of neighbors not just fellow dwellers. Cleveland was a planned community, a vision of the Connecticut Land Company, which owned the vast Western Reserve abutting the state of Connecticut. In 1796, visionaries of the company sought to create a New England village and early Cleveland reflected this effort. Cleveland, with its church spires and homogenous population, appeared to be transplanted from the adjoining region. But waves of immigration followed the construction of the Ohio-Erie Canal.[1] Irish and Germans began the process in the 1820s. One hundred years later, nearly a third of the 796,841 Clevelanders were foreign born.[2] Over fifty ethnic groups were represented. Neighborhoods developed, each dominated by an ethnic or racial group.

By the early 1950s Cleveland had made the shift to a more urban rather than rural community. The Cuyahoga River brought with it commerce that led the city to become a bustling hub of business in the Midwest. Even today the Cuyahoga assists the city as a commercial mainstay in the Midwest region. But as Cleveland became distinctly urban, so did its problems. Crime was one by-product, but it was small in scale and violence in comparison to other Midwestern urban areas such as Chicago. The growth of Cleveland was manageable, and heretofore, so was the growing criminal element.

Cleveland had made headlines for its crime and crime fighting before. In the 1930s the renowned safety director, Eliot Ness, had fought organized crime in Cleveland. Ness was determined to eliminate the vice of illegal liquor from the streets of Cleveland. Ness's tactics were highly publicized and his successes were detailed in newspapers around the country. The youngest safety director in the city's history, Ness fought crime until the repeal of Prohibition. However, Ness's successes were like a mere finger in the dike, staving off what seemed inevitable. Cleveland could not keep out criminal enterprise indefinitely.

---

[1]   D. Van Tassel and John J. Grabowski, eds. *Cleveland: A Tradition of Reform* (Cleveland: Kent State University Press, 1986), p. 3.

[2]   Van Tassel and Grabowski, p. 4.

The special unit that included Delau and his partner, Michael Haney, was established to combat the growing numbers games in Cleveland. The officers focused on two games of chance: clearinghouse, or what was sometimes called numbers, and policy. Numbers and policy were played almost exclusively by blacks, primarily because the minimum bet could be as small as a few pennies and could be waged often, even daily. As Prohibition waned as a source of lucrative profit, whites turned their attention to gambling as a means of income. To do so meant driving blacks out of the business. The struggle for control took on interesting forms—raids, shootings, and bombings.[3] Gambling was the leading "vice for profit" criminal business. The numbers were not trivial, the dollar amount being in the thousands per day. Both Delau and Haney became experts on these games of chance, and each would often testify in court about how these forms of gambling were conducted. The special unit was successful in curtailing the rackets by keeping whites and the mafia from taking over an illegal activity dominated by blacks. Their job became twofold—keeping the peace between encroaching whites and black gamblers while snuffing out altogether games of chance.

Clearinghouse, or numbers, is similar to the present legal lottery in the state of Ohio. In Cleveland in the 1950s, "players" selected a number between 000 and 999. They could place a bet of as little as a single penny and up to two dollars. The numbers were selected from the stocks and bonds tallies in the Cleveland newspaper, the *Cleveland News*.

Players would then place their bet with a "writer." This person collected wagers from many players and accumulated hundreds of dollars by the end of the day. For this effort, the writer kept 25 percent of the wagers as compensation. Between 1:30 and 3:00 o'clock in the afternoon, the monies collected by the numbers writer, less the 25 percent, were given to a "pick-up" person. The pick-up met the writer at a given location and then proceeded to

---

[3]   Michael Roberts, "Why They Blew Shondor Birns Away," *Cleveland Magazine*, July/December 1975, p. 56.

meet various other writers to obtain their written wagers. The pick-up could rendezvous with several dozen writers during the day. Eventually the pick-up met with a trusted representative of the clearinghouse operator and turned over all the wagers. This person then proceeded to the "office" where the clearinghouse operator and his closest and most trusted workers tallied the monies and determined the winners and payoffs. The operator might or might not be present. These five to eight office workers totaled the wagers accumulated by each writer and noted the amount on the end of the adding machine tape. Then they recorded the amount of bets turned in by each pick-up person and calculated his or her compensation of 10 percent. By four or four-thirty in the afternoon all the tapes were tallied and the winning numbers selected. The clearinghouse workers consulted the financial section of the newspaper, which contained, and still does, a compilation of action on the market entitled,"What the Market Did." Reading down the first two columns of "Advances," "Declines," and "Unchanged," the winning numbers for stocks and bonds were derived. If there were any winners, the numbers were noted on the adding machine tape and one copy was given to the pick-up person to initiate the payoff to the player.

The other popular game of chance was policy. This game, too, allowed small bets, which were commonly one, five, or ten cents. Two versions of policy were played, one during the day and the other in the evening. The game was played the same; what differed was the odds, which were more lucrative in the night house. Some players placed their bets with writers similar to clearinghouse. But policy had a social aspect to it. Players, often the elderly, would gather at policy drawing locations like bingo parlors. These policy parlors had the feel of speakeasies during Prohibition. Players would spend the afternoon there, placing bets and lingering about to see the results.

Betting required much conversation, since a method of selection was involved. "Players" would wager on numbers between 1 and 68 during the day and 1 and 100 in the evening. The selections were often based on superstition or personal quirk. Bettors could even select their bets from what was referred to as the "dream book." Whatever your dream or superstition—death was 769, dirt was 369—you could consult the dream book and bet accordingly. This book was referred to by those who felt that a dream they had the night before, or an event that happened to them, signaled a particular way in which to wager. One well-known criminal often told Officer Haney that he bet 258, Haney's badge number. On one occasion a player at the policy house at 55th and Central bet 769, the "death" number. He died that very day. People were astonished. The coincidence was no coincidence; consequently, the dream book was a hot seller.[4]

Once bets were placed with a writer or in a policy house, a "puller" would select twelve balls from a bag. Players could win by choosing a "side" or a "flat," meaning that they selected two numbers sequentially (a side, which paid better odds) or selected several of the winning numbers regardless of order (a flat). The drawn numbers were posted on result sheets.

The game was corrupt. Policy operators subtly kept the winnings down by using balls that were either convex or concave. Pullers were instructed to rarely draw a side of "hot numbers," those that players selected often. These numbers had a different feel to them, so while the draw appeared random, it was quite calculated. Flats were more common. There were always winners, so complaints of foul play were reduced to mere grumbles. The winning numbers were recorded on two-by-six-inch tape, or "policy slips," and stamped with sequential serial numbers. These were then taken back along with the winnings and distributed to players.

There were very few operators who ran both clearinghouse and policy. The networks were too vast. There were six to eight clearinghouse operators and about eight to ten policy houses. For example, California Gold, Mound Bayou, T & O, S & G, and Interstate all operated in Cleveland during the 1950s and

---

[4]   Telephone interview with Officer Michael Haney by the author, November 17, 1992.

early 1960s. These games of chance were lucrative. One operator known to Haney and Delau cleared a profit of nearly $20,000 a day.[5]

~~~

At the epicenter of the Cleveland numbers and policy games was Shondor Birns. Notorious in Cleveland for his use of "muscle" in the criminal community, Shondor Birns made a grand play to control policy. "Shin-do," as terrified blacks pronounced his name, was a white Jewish immigrant who was a legend in Cleveland for being tough, smart, and powerful. Birns, a dapper dresser, often clutching an expensive cigar, looked like a gangster sent from central casting in Hollywood. It was hard to imagine Birns did anything else, with his wide lapels, expensive double-breasted pinstriped suits, and wide-brimmed fedoras. He looked like a gangster, not what you might picture as an executive of Cleveland's Union Supply and Towel Company, as he claimed. Birns was the real thing.

Shon Birns played on the greed of competing racketeers by creating and organizing a system that allowed everyone to share in the profits. It also reduced the size of payoffs to winners by controlling the fluctuating odds. Numbers operators would often increase their odds in an attempt to lure business away from other operators. The result of such undercutting practices was often violence. Birns offered to "keep the peace" between the clearinghouses, control the odds, and cover any payoff that was too large for an operator to handle. This arrangement would curtail competition between clearinghouses and increase profits. Regulating the competition, providing insurance coverage for high payoffs, and control of the house odds came at a price. Birns would provide these "keeping the peace" services for 25 percent of the business. He was to be paid a weekly "fee," $200 per operator per week. It

---

[5]   This entire section is the result of several interviews and correspondence with Officer Haney and Officer Delau. The interviews took place separately, and it is amazing, despite the passage of time, the similarity of their statements.

seemed a small price to pay for some certainty within the gaming business.

One particular clearinghouse operator, Donald "The Kid" King, had tired of the arrangement with Birns. In December 1956 he lowered his payment from the required $200 to $100 a week. By February of 1957 he had quit paying altogether. King felt that Birns did little for the money and that King could negotiate with the other clearinghouses himself. Birns's services were no longer necessary. The last meeting of Birns and King was on May 5th, fifteen days before King's home was bombed. After Shondor Birns spotted King on Kinsman Road, Birns took King for a drive, informing him along the way that he had to fulfill his commitments. Birns expected payment, but King begged off.

When Donald King lost his front porch early that May morning, he knew who likely would do such a thing. Shondor Birns's trademark tool of enforcement was the bomb.[6] In the late 1940s Joe Allen, a clearinghouse operator, found his 1947 Cadillac blown up in his driveway. Allen accused Birns, who had previously suggested that Allen hire him to insure the peace in policy. Allen had rejected the idea and Birns had noted that he needed the protection against neighborhood explosions. Birns was acquitted of the bombing charges but was subsequently accused of tampering with the jury. He was later retried and acquitted. Birns's enforcement tool of bombing became his signature, his calling card. "Birns used so many bombs over the years that police credited him with turning explosives into a new criminal art form."[7] Ironically, Birns would meet his end in 1975 by way of a car bomb.

King immediately fingered Birns as the perpetrator. "Shondor was one of the five pistols who bombed me," King told the press.[8] King cooperated fully with the police, telling them that he was one of five clearinghouse operators who paid Birns $200 a week. King had not paid Birns since early spring. He was out of the numbers business, he claimed. Donald King went on to name the

---

[6]   *Cleveland Magazine*, July/December 1975, p. 83.

[7]   Ibid.

[8]   *The Cleveland Press*, Monday May 20, 1957, p. 1.

four other numbers operators, Edward Keeling, Dan Boone, Buckeye Jackson, and Thomas Turk as possible suspects. He named Elijah Abercrombie as the person who collected the weekly money for Birns.[9] King told the police everything, though they already knew about Birns and the others.

Less than three hours after the bombing, the police arrested Alex Shondor Birns at his Judson Avenue home. He told the police nothing more than his address, telephone number, and his place of employment, Union Towel and Supply Company on 34th Street. Birns, out of federal prison for only eight months, denied the charges saying, "I don't know these guys and I don't want to know them. They tell the police anything and the police believe them. I've got a job and a family."[10] Since Birns had returned to Cleveland there had been two murders and seven bombings of policy figures.[11] Birns proclaimed his innocence, calling King a liar.

Carl Delau then arrested Keeling, Boone, Jackson, and Turk and took them to Central Station for questioning, but he gained little information. Working in the Bureau of Special Investigation, Delau was well versed in the clearinghouse business. He knew that Birns was attempting to put a new system in place for determining the winning stock number in policy. King had resisted. None of the four who were arrested with Birns had anything nice to say about King, and all of them sidestepped their association with Shondor Birns. Jackson told Delau that King was "just a kid" and that King was lying. The five were charged with blackmail on May 21, 1957, but the police had few leads other than their only cooperating source, Donald King. On May 25, 1957, the front page of the *Call and Post* blared the headline, "King Spills All to Cops: Blows Lid off Numbers Muscle."

By the time of trial in the fall of 1957, Donald King was being pressured to not testify against Birns. Without King, the only witness, the charges would more than likely be dropped. As King told the story, he was at home playing

---

9   Cleveland Police Report filed by Sgt. Carl I. Delau, May 21, 1957.
10   "Birns Is Jailed in Bombing Charge," *Cleveland Press*, May 20, 1957.
11   Roberts, *Cleveland Magazine* July/December 1975, p. 87.

cards one evening in early October prior to the Birns trial. He went outside to his car to retrieve some things from the glove compartment. As he walked toward the parked car in his garage, he heard some movement coming from the bushes. Knowing instantly that this meant trouble, King turned and ran. Donald King barely missed the full brunt of the shotgun blast that quickly followed. Lucky for King, the only damage to him was cosmetic. Some thirty pellets from a twelve-gauge shotgun struck him in the back of the head. King's neck and head were peppered with pellets. The damage was superficial, yet some of the blasted pellets created holes in his ears large enough to see through. For a year or so after the incident Donald King would extract pellets from the back of his neck, a not so subtle reminder of the incident.

Despite the overt threat, King did testify against Birns when he was brought to trial in October of 1957. Donald King, the star witness, spoke so quickly and in such an animated manner that the jury could hardly understand him. The press nicknamed Donald "The Kid" King, "The Talker," "The Mouth," "The Canary." On the witness stand, the defense attorney forced King to admit that he was a numbers operator as well as the owner of an illicit liquor store. King was the only witness, and not a particularly sympathetic one. The trial ended in a hung jury of eleven to one. The state decided to not retry Birns and the charges were eventually dropped. Later it was revealed that Birns purchased the hanging vote of the jury for $8,000. To make matters even worse for King, the Internal Revenue Service promptly filed charges against King for nonpayment of taxes in regard to his gambling profits and placed a lien on his home. The house at East 151st Street was seized by the government as collateral for nonpayment.[12] So Birns eluded any legal sanction while King, embarrassed, publically exposed, and now in legal trouble, faced jail time and financial woes for not paying Birns a mere $200 per week.

---

[12]   Christopher Evans, "The Man Who Would Be King," *Cleveland Plain Dealer Magazine*, October 23, 1988.

~~~

By May of 1957 the nine justices of the United States Supreme Court were in the stage of the term that could only be described as grueling. Since October of 1956 they had docketed cases and heard them in court Monday through Wednesday, 10:00 A.M. to 3:00 P.M., during the first half of each month. By April they shifted their concentration from oral arguments to completing the written opinions that would eventually be handed down before their recess, near the end of June. Then would come a brief summer rest before the entire process would begin again.

The 1956 term, as it was called, was significant, marking the beginning of change that was to affect the status and reputation of the Warren Court. Earl Warren, Chief Justice since 1953, was coming into his own. Warren, a politician, had not donned a judicial robe in his life before becoming the fourteenth Chief Justice of the United States. He had served as a state attorney general, a governor, and even a candidate for vice president with Thomas Dewey, losing to Truman in 1948. His lack of judicial experience was a target for coaptation by the two legal giants who dominated the Court, Felix Frankfurter and Hugo Black. Felix Frankfurter, a long-time Harvard law professor, attempted to teach the new Chief Justice about the "proper" judicial role, that of restraint. Frankfurter believed that the judiciary was an institution of last resort, not a policy maker such as the two other branches of government. Small, compact, abrupt, and forthright, Frankfurter was intellectually arrogant, yet brilliant. He was known for occasionally lecturing the Brethren about the case at hand. These diatribes usually lasted fifty minutes, the length of a typical Harvard Law School lecture. Frankfurter's intellectual skills were evident, but his personality and interpersonal skills, or lack of them, created tension and alienated some of his colleagues. Frankfurter was prickly, and consequently working with him was often a challenge. But his vision of the role of the judiciary, a maintenance of the status quo and a resolve to let the democratic process lead the country for good or ill, made some sense.

Frankfurter's intellectual enemy was Hugo Black, the leader of the Court's progressive wing, which believed that the judiciary was under constitutional obligation to respond to social change and need. Black, the former United States senator, was Franklin Roosevelt's first appointment to the bench after the great court-packing battle of 1936. Roosevelt selected the slow-talking Alabamian for his literalist reading of the Constitution. Black believed that the Constitution should have a contemporary meaning, so much so that non-lawyers would be able to understand it. Law shouldn't be a set of hieroglyphics that could only be translated by judges with special skills and understanding. Law and its meaning should be self-evident for all. What mattered was what the words of the Constitution meant to the man on the street, not what the Framers of the Constitution meant almost two centuries ago. If law was to respond to the need of society it would have to be read in a contemporary light. Black believed law could be read quite literally. Words did not connote hidden meanings that only judges could decipher. Black would later give what is now a famous interview with Eric Severeid in which an elderly, yet quite animated Justice Black holds up his crumpled copy of the Constitution and declares that he would often refer back to the literal words and meaning of the text. If the Constitution says "Congress shall make no law" for example, then Congress shall not, according to Black. Simple and direct.

By the spring of 1957 Warren's formulation of his own judicial philosophy was near complete. The struggle for his "judicial soul" had been won, and along with Black and William Douglas, Warren would embrace judicial activism, the antithesis of Frankfurter's judicial restraint. Warren felt that the Court must play a role in the fundamental and enduring liberty of American society. It must react, especially as the other branches of government were deadlocked and bogged down. The court had paid a dear price for such a stance. On the heels of the two *Brown* decisions,[13] the Court to many looked like a

---

13   *Brown v. The Board of Education of Topeka, Kansas*, 347 U.S. 483 (1954), *Brown v. The Board of Education of Topeka, Kansas*, 349 U.S. 294 (1955).

"superlegislature." Billboards proclaiming "Impeach Earl Warren" sprang up across the United States. A bill was introduced in Congress to impeach the entire Supreme Court. Congress used the power of the purse to deny the Justices a pay raise or budget increase. The normally reactive institution appeared to be proactive and leading the charge for change.

The Court was changing in other ways as well. The nine justices who began the Court's work would not be the same nine by term's end. These personnel changes contributed to marked differences of the Court. Charles Whittaker would replace Stanley Reed, and the Chief would gain his closest ally and kindred spirit in the newly appointed William Brennan. Brennan, a former New Jersey Supreme Court judge, was the first member of the Court to be born in the twentieth century. Along with Black and Douglas, Warren and his new lieutenant, Brennan, who ironically was Felix Frankfurter's student at Harvard Law School, would begin the shift toward an activist posture on the Court. Harold Burton, Tom Clark, and the second John Marshall Harlan rounded out the Court and one or more of them was often influenced by the Black, Douglas, Warren, Brennan alliance.

~~~

Numbers running was labor intensive. It required hiring people to make drop-offs and pickups, as well as bookkeepers, tabulators, look outs, collectors, and strongmen. The army of workers grew as clearinghouses became more and more profitable. Dollree (Doll-ray) Mapp worked occasionally for both Donald King and Shondor Birns, making drops, pickups, and sometimes keeping books. The police knew that she was involved in policy. When staking out known clearinghouses, they would regularly record license plates and later run them through the Department of Motor Vehicles' computer to obtain the name of the owners. Dollree Mapp's name had come up regularly. The police also knew her for her striking appearance. Dolly was a beautiful woman who Delau described as "foxy." She was tall, shapely, and dressed with a flair, making her a standout in any crowd. Her appearance was striking. Even by today's standards, pictures of her show a beauty that is timeless. She was classically handsome and she knew it. Her looks took her a long way. Men, both white and black, found her attractive, and she took advantage of the opportunities these relationships provided her. She had some formal schooling but her intellectual assets fell into the realm of street-smart rather than a bookish formal education. Her education had come from using her physical attributes and her quick wit to advance through those she knew. She had married once, to Jimmy Bivens, a professional boxer. She later became the girlfriend of Archie Moore, the famed heavyweight boxer who once fought Joe Louis. Dolly knew Shondor Birns well and years later referred to him with a softened voice as "Shon." Combining her physical beauty with her streetwise savvy, Dollree Mapp, while on the periphery, was a player in Cleveland's vice trade. For a black woman in the 1950s, she had made her mark. Carl Delau stated over thirty years later that she was the smartest black woman he had ever known.[14] On more than one occasion, he stated she was brilliant.

Carl Delau and Dollree Mapp had met on a number of occasions. Delau had once encountered Dolly in downtown Cleveland. Delau and his partner, Michael Haney, noticed her car near 150th Street and Wilbur. Dolly must have noticed them too because shortly after they began trailing her, policy slips began flying from her open car windows. Hundreds of them sailed out onto the streets of Cleveland. Delau and Haney pulled her over. While Haney began gathering up the scattered policy slips, Delau approached the car and asked Dolly Mapp about the clearinghouse slips that had departed her car in such haste. Mapp stated coyly but defiantly that she "knew nothing" about the policy slips Officer Haney was now presenting to her. Delau asked her to get out of the car, sensing that she was sitting on a pile of slips. Dolly remarked that if he wanted to see what she was sitting on, he could go with her to her apartment and see for himself. The sexual overtone was amusing but clearly not what

---

[14]   Interview with Carl I. Delau , Cleveland, Ohio, August 14, 1992.

Delau had in mind. He again asked her to step out of the car. A search of the trunk turned up an adding machine, an ordinary tool of the trade for the numbers racket.[15] Dollree Mapp was taken to Central Station on May 28, 1954, and booked for possession of clearinghouse slips and paraphernalia. She was fined $100 and court costs. So the beautiful black woman who was involved in the policy and numbers business had her first mug shot taken. The picture shows Dolly Mapp unadorned, holding a rectangular police department sign with the booking number 89632. The picture reveals an almost rundown Dolly Mapp, not so cocky and coy as the one Delau had encountered with policy slips streaming out her car windows. This meeting on the streets of Cleveland in May of 1954 was not her first encounter with Sergeant Delau or the police, and it would not be her last.

---

[15]   This same story was recounted separately and independently by both Officers Carl Delau and Michael Haney. Interview conducted by the author with Delau, Cleveland, Ohio, August 14, 1992. Interview conducted by the author with Haney via telephone, November 17, 1992.

CHAPTER TWO
Search and Seizure

The weather reports on the front page of the *Call and Post*, the *Plain Dealer*, and the *Cleveland Press* all differed slightly on telling the locals what to expect weatherwise on May 23, 1957. The *Plain Dealer* projected the temperature to be 75 degrees. The *Cleveland Press* anticipated the weather to be much the same but cloudy. However, the *Call and Post*, the newspaper of choice of Cleveland's black community, reported that afternoon and evening showers were expected with a chance of thunderstorms. Such a pessimistic report was prophetic for a particular Clevelander residing on Milverton Road.

On Thursday, May 23rd, three days after the bombing of Donald King's home, Carl Delau and his partner, Michael Haney, were still searching for clues to link Shondor Birns to the crime. In the early afternoon, Officer Jackson of the sixth district received an anonymous telephone call informing the sergeant on duty that one of the individuals the police suspected in the bombing, someone they wanted to question, was hiding out at 14705 Milverton Road. The caller also informed Jackson that the police would find a large amount of policy paraphernalia hidden in the home. The information was passed along to Delau and Haney, who were riding with Patrolman Michael Dever.

The address was familiar. The three officers left downtown Cleveland, taking Euclid Avenue near University Circle and Case Western Reserve University. Winding through Little Italy, at approximately 1:30 P.M., Delau, Haney, and Dever pulled their marked squad car in front of the home of Dollree Mapp. The car in the driveway was familiar too: it appeared to be that of Virgil

Ogletree.[1] Ogletree had done time for numbers, extortion, policy, and clearinghouse. He was working with Edward Keeling in numbers and had a reputation for conducting some of the more unsavory business of Shondor Birns. The officers did not believe that Ogletree bombed Don King's home but felt he could probably give them information that would assist them in finding out who did.

Dollree Mapp's home was a two-story brick house in the Shaker Heights section of Cleveland. Most of the homes along Milverton Road were modest structures with a similarity among them that indicated the entire neighborhood had been built from more or less the same blueprint. The home, which appeared to be a single-family dwelling, was actually split into two apartments, one upstairs and one downstairs, with a driveway on the left side leading to a garage. Dollree occupied the upstairs with her teenage daughter Barbara Bivens, the child she once shared with her former husband, boxer Jimmy Bivens. The downstairs apartment was rented to Minerva Tate.[2]

Delau and Haney parked and walked up the drive while Dever went to the front of the home. Delau rang the doorbell located near the side-door nameplate "Mapp." Instead of coming to the door, Dollree Mapp coyly opened the upper window near the driveway and inquired what the officers wanted. Recounting this event in separate discussions over thirty years later, both Haney and Delau

---

[1] Virgil Ogletree's troubles did not end in 1957. He was arrested in 1992 on cocaine possession charges and sentenced to prison. In an interview with Dollree Mapp by the author, Mapp mentioned that she was returning to Cleveland soon and would see Ogletree. Apparently their friendship has endured.

[2] Detective Haney told the author that he believed that the confidential informer who called the police was Minerva Tate. She was acquainted with Officer Jackson and later told the police that she believed Ogletree and a great deal of policy paraphernalia were located in the Mapp home. One police officer told the author that Don King was the source, because he knew Dollree's former tenant at the time, Morris Jones, and felt that he might possibly be involved in the bombing of King's home.

said, "I can remember her calling down from the window as if it were yesterday."[3]

"What do you want?" she asked them.

"Hello Dolly. We just wanted to come in and take a quick look around," Delau replied casually.

"Why do you want to come inside? What are you looking for?" she inquired.

Delau didn't exactly know. He certainly wanted to question Ogletree, but beyond that he wasn't sure. These officers knew Dolly Mapp participated in numbers, at least on the fringe. Her car was regularly seen at gaming houses. There was a possibility, as the anonymous caller had insinuated, that they would find evidence of illegal gambling. In fact the police believed that the Mapp house was the location for the California Gold policyhouse.[4] Delau wasn't sure how to respond to Dollree Mapp.

Mapp continued to inquire, now more sarcastically, what Delau wanted in her home. Delau told her nothing concrete. After several more minutes of conversation she said: "I'll call my attorney and see if he thinks I should let you in." Mapp in fact did call the office of her lawyer, A. L. Kearns. She had recently retained Kearns to file a civil suit against her former boyfriend, boxer Archie Moore. The lawsuit appeared to be an attempt to extract money. Mapp charged Moore with breach of promise for refusing to marry her. Mapp eventually dropped the charges and whether Mapp profited financially from the legal maneuver is unclear. Kearns was not available to speak to Mapp so Dolly was put through to one of his partners, Walter Green. Green was a relatively young lawyer whose specialty was not criminal matters and her request was not something with which he was readily familiar.

"Do the police have a search warrant?" he asked.

"I don't know. I didn't ask," she replied.

---

3   Interviews with Delau and Haney, various dates in 1992, 1993.
4   *Cleveland Plain Dealer*, May 24, 1957.

"Well, don't let them in unless they show you a search warrant, but if they do, you will have to admit them," counseled Green.

It turns out that Green's advice was not correct, at least not in the practice of American criminal law in 1957. While the constitutional principle of search warrant usage existed, the common practice under Ohio law was that search warrants were rarely used. Only when raids were planned well in advance were warrants considered. Most lawful searches occurred without search warrants. Green later recalled, "If I had known the way the law worked, I might have told her that she might as well open up the door."[5] Nevertheless, based on Green's instructions, Mapp asked Officers Delau and Haney whether or not they had a search warrant. The officers had not anticipated such inquiries and hemmed and hawed before admitting that they did not have a warrant with them but clearly could get one. Miss Mapp suggest they do so, and with that, closed the door, leaving the three officers stymied on her front steps.

The Fourth Amendment to the United States Constitution reads: "The right of the people to be secure in their persons, houses, papers, and effects, against unreasonable searches and seizures, shall not be violated, and no Warrants shall issue, but upon probable cause, supported by Oath or affirmation, and particularly describing the place to be searched, and the persons or things to be seized." Despite the asserted need for a search warrant, the common practice in Cleveland and many other cities in the United States was to search without a warrant. If the police had enough clues and evidence to send them to a citizen's door, it was common to follow through on those leads. Delau and Haney had conducted hundreds of searches without warrants, and their searches were routinely upheld in court as lawful. Delau recounted for me years later, "I cannot remember a time when we searched the wrong person or did not find what we suspected. We did not search as fishing expeditions but as a result of

---

5   Jethro K. Lieberman, *Milestones: 200 Years of American Law* (New York: Oxford University Press, 1976), p. 283.

investigations that led us to a location."[6] The resulting search was fruitful.

The request by Delau and Haney to enter Dollree Mapp's home and search was not uncommon or extraordinary. It was not deemed outrageous or gross behavior. This was standard operating procedure for these two Cleveland cops. In fact, it was standard operating procedure for almost every local police officer in America. Nevertheless, when Dolly informed Delau and Haney that they would have to produce a warrant to enter her home they set about the task of getting one. Warrants were not commonplace but they were used. Delau and company drove away, finding a nearby pay phone. Carl Delau called Sergeant Cooney and gave him the specifics. He gave Cooney Mapp's home address and what they suspected they might find inside, both in terms of the King bombing and clearinghouse materials. Cooney said he would take care of the warrant. Unbeknownst to Delau until much later, here was where the critical error was committed.

Very few police officers were familiar with the procedures for obtaining a search warrant. The process was used so infrequently that most officers had never secured one as a predicate to a search. A preplanned raid was usually handled by a desk officer who was more familiar with the paperwork of policing than a street patrolman. Sergeant Cooney asked Lieutenant Tommy White to set about getting a warrant to search Mapp's home. This entailed drawing up an affidavit that stated what evidence of criminal activity that police suspected would be found at the place or person to be searched. Warrants sometimes specified a person who the police suspected was at a specific locale. Other times an affidavit noted material evidence that the police wanted to obtain. The specific details would be laid out clearly in the affidavit, which was then presented to a judge. The judge, a neutral and impartial magistrate, would read the affidavit and determine if the police had probable cause. Probable cause, the legal threshold to support a search, requires an

---

[6]   Telephone interview by the author with Carl Delau, 1995.

educated and reasonable conclusion that an allegation is well founded.[7] If the standard is met, the judge then authorizes a search warrant that is drawn up by a clerk and given to the police.

This procedure was not done regularly for many reasons. Occasionally a suspect was "tipped off" by someone that a warrant was being processed. The police would then show up to conduct a search only to find the criminals well prepared for their arrival, the element of surprise taken away. Some of the tipoffs were a result of corruption within city hall. Big-city criminals were savvy and knew that clerks and administrative staffs had information vital to them. Salaries of police officers and other civic workers were low enough that bribes were tempting. In addition, most police felt the procedure of obtaining warrants was cumbersome and a hindrance to law enforcement. Why follow such arduous rules if not absolutely required to? Most of all, the extra step of securing a search warrant seemed to tip the scales of justice in favor of the criminal. An officer's belief of wrongdoing was not enough: a judge would have to concur and grant permission to search.

What existed in Cleveland at the time was a culture of avoiding such steps, classifying them as an unfair advantage to the criminal. Thus few in the police department knew how to obtain search warrants. When warrants were sought, Cooney typically asked Officer John Ungarvy to obtain them. On this particular day he was apparently unavailable and the job fell to Lieutenant White.

After telephoning Cooney, Delau and Haney returned to Mapp's home, believing the search warrant was en route. The three officers waited in their patrolcar for the warrant to be delivered. Mapp, still perched in her upstairs window, could see the police down the street. She called her lawyer again, telling him what she saw from her window. Delau and Haney advised

---

[7]   What is and is not probable cause, while seemingly simple and straightforward, is in practice more complicated. Judges must consider the reputation of the police involved, anonymous sources, exigencies, and a myriad of factors. The basic evidence must point to the likelihood of finding materials or persons that indicate or support criminal wrongdoing.

headquarters of events and waited. Dollree advised her attorney and did the same.

By about four o'clock in the afternoon "Lieutenant White arrived on the scene with a search warrant."[8] There were now at least seven police officers outside the Mapp house on Milverton Road. The officers on the scene proceeded accordingly. Again they sought admittance.

The fact that all parties had knowledge of a search warrant is undisputed. At the time the search was conducted all the police officers involved believed that a search warrant was obtained; Mapp's attorney, and initially even Mapp herself, believed that the police were operating with a search warrant. Ironically, no one thought to look to see if the piece of paper so commented on, so significant to future events and American constitutional law, was indeed a warrant to search 14705 Milverton Road, the home of Dollree Mapp. This act of omission is, without a doubt, significant. The very piece of paper at the heart of what would become *Dollree Mapp v. The State of Ohio* wasn't even scrutinized by any of the principal players. All took it for granted that the paper brought to the scene by Lieutenant White was an official search warrant to conduct a search of Dollree Mapp's home for a material witness in the King bombing and for potential possession of gambling paraphernalia. The trifoliate document remained folded, unopened.

Dollree Mapp did not immediately answer the door, and the record reflects that at least one of the several doors to the house was forcibly opened. Carl Delau testified in court that "we did pry the screen door to gain entrance." Walter Green, Mapp's attorney, testified that a policeman "tried to kick in the door" and then "broke the glass in the door and somebody reached in and opened the door and let them in." Mapp testified that "the back door was broken." According to Justice Douglas's concurrence in the Supreme Court

---

[8]   This is the most critical divergence of facts. This statement is taken from the Motion to Dismiss from the brief of the State of Ohio in the Supreme Court of the United States. The officers testified that Lieutenant White obtained a search warrant. According to A. L. Kearns, the officers on the scene were told that a search warrant had been obtained.

decision in 1961, "For the next two and a half hours, the police laid siege to the house." It is interesting to note that the State's Motion to Dismiss before the high court states that "there was no evidence that any of the incriminating evidence was taken from the home of the Appellant by the use of any brutal or offensive physical force against the Appellant."[9]

At the time of their entry, Mapp was halfway down the stairs coming toward the front door. She demanded to see the search warrant, noting that the police had had none on their earlier attempt at admittance. One of the officers, Lieutenant White, waived a piece of paper in Mapp's face, indicating that it was the search warrant, which legalized their search. Mapp grabbed the paper and placed it down the front of her dress. The police then restrained her and recovered the so-called warrant.

The record of the Court of Common Pleas states that

> there is considerable doubt as to whether there ever was any warrant for the search of the defendant's home. No warrant was offered in evidence; there was no testimony as to who issued any warrant or as to what any warrant contained, and the absence from evidence of any such warrant is not explained or otherwise accounted for in the record. There is nothing in the record tending to prove or from which an inference may be drawn that there was a warrant, and no one has ever suggested that any warrant that we may assume there may have been described anything other than policy paraphernalia as things to be searched for.[10]

What is important to note is that *at the time* all believed the paper was indeed a search warrant. Only later was the existence of a warrant doubted. On May 23, 1957, everyone, including Dollree Mapp and Carl Delau, believed that a search warrant was the basis for the search of Mapp's home.

The supplemental brief for the state of Ohio says that during the trial the defense never requested the state to produce the search warrant or prove its existence. The police who conducted the search testified that they did not

[9]   Motion to Suppress, Brief of the State of Ohio, Supreme Court of Ohio.
[10]   From *Mapp v. Ohio* in the Supreme Court of Ohio, 170 Ohio St. 427, 430.

obtain a search warrant themselves but awaited Lieutenant White, who was to appear with the search warrant. While waiting they did nothing. When he arrived, they attempted to execute the search, and Mapp resisted. The trial record reflects no questions about whether Lieutenant White actually obtained a search warrant. The appellant, Dollree Mapp, did not subpoena Lieutenant White. The state of Ohio did not introduce his testimony, admitting only that no proper search warrant was secured, not that one did not exist.

Because she "was belligerent in resisting the official rescue of the 'warrant' from her person," the officers handcuffed Mapp to another officer.[11] She was then taken to her bedroom and forced to sit on the bed. Carl Delau later said that the reason for this was to negate any claim that the police stole items from her.

The police made a complete and thorough search of the four-room flat as well as the basement. They searched a dresser, chest of drawers, a closet, and suitcases. They searched the child's bedroom, the living room, the kitchen, and even photo albums and personal papers. The entire second floor was searched.

The police then searched the basement. From a trunk, materials deemed to be obscene were seized. This material was considered lewd and lascivious, and when confronted, Mapp claimed she found the items while cleaning. She asserted that the material belonged to a former boarder, a Morris Jones. She had agreed to store his belonging until his return and had no knowledge of the contents of the trunk. The obscene material included four pamphlets, several photographs, and a pencil doodle. In addition, Officer Haney found in her bedroom dresser *The Affairs of the Troubadour, Little Darlings, London Stage*

---

[11]   The jurisdictional statement says that she was handcuffed to the stairway banister. Again there is dispute in the record of whether Mapp was handcuffed to the banister or not. The argument statement of the Motion to Dismiss before the Supreme Court of the U.S. p. 6 states that Mapp was not handcuffed to the banister. It does not say she wasn't handcuffed, just not handcuffed to the banister. A police officer then "grabbed" her and, "twisted her hand." Mapp "yelled and pleaded with him" because "it was hurting" (all from *U.S. Reports*, p. 645).

Affairs, and *Memories of a Hotel Man.* Upon seizure of these items, Mapp replied: "Better not look at those; they might excite you."[12] In a suitcase by the bed, Officer Haney found a hand drawn penciled picture.[13] Sergeant Delau found four groups of obscene photographs.[14] California Gold policy was found in large quantities.

Here is where the versions of events diverge. By some accounts, the search of Mapp's home is brutal and frightening. A window is broken, the occupant handcuffed, and the search seemingly endless. Other reports indicate that the police broke one pane of a glass door, since the occupant would not provide access, and conducted a thorough yet reasonable search. History, too, has embellished the search of Dollree Mapp, making it extraordinary. Upon review, it is doubtful that it was. She was a notable Cleveland figure and a personality. A beautiful woman, she was linked to two well-known local celebrities (Jimmy Bivens and Archie Moore) as well as members of Cleveland's crime community (Donald King, Shondor Birns, and Virgil Ogletree). The bombing of King's home was sensational because it involved infighting in Cleveland's underworld. Yet looking back the search was no different than many others. That is not to suggest that it did not cross the line between legal and nonlegal, but to make clear that the line did not lie where it does today. The search of Mapp's home was standard procedure in 1957. What is different is not the actions of Delau and Haney but *the reaction* of the Supreme Court of the United States. Whether or not one agrees with the eventual outcome of the Mapp decision of 1961, the events of May 23, 1957, are routine for the day. But times were changing, and "routine" would take on quite a different meaning in the future.

After the search and the seizure of the pornographic items, Dollree Mapp was arrested, taken to the police station, and jailed. Dollree Mapp would defend

---

[12] Motion to Dismiss from State of Ohio before the Supreme Court of the United States.

[13] State's exhibits 6, 7, 8, 9 and 5.

[14] State exhibits 10, 11, 12, 13.

the possession of pornography by arguing it was not hers. She had rented out the spare room to a boarder (Jones) who was now residing in New York. Sergeant Delau testified that the room in which he found obscene materials did not contain men's clothing but seemed to be inhabited by a female. Despite Mapp's assertion that the obscene material did not belong to her, there was little evidence of ownership by another. Mapp's feeble argument did nothing to mitigate the seriousness of the offense.

Ohio law made this distinction moot. Mere possession of obscene material was punishable by seven years in prison. It did not matter that the possessor was not the owner, so Mapp's argument made little difference. The books and pamphlets themselves were vulgar. In recalling their discovery of these items, both Haney and Delau expressed their disgust with contorted faces that looked as if they had eaten the sourest of lemons.

Mapp would later argue that Officers Haney and Delau did not find books and pictures in her room but planted them there. She said that the pencil drawings were in her suitcase but that they belonged to Jones. She had packed away some of this things. "There was no evidence produced at the trial by the defense that any belongings of one Morris Jones were in the home at the time, other than a cosmetology book purportedly belonging to Jones and claimed to have been in the suitcase."[15]

Mapp never disputed that the material was obscene; only that it was not hers and not "in her possession or under her control" as meant in the Ohio Statutes 2905.34. She found the items in question and packed them into a box and into one of her suitcases to put into storage. She claimed that she never looked at these books and pictures again before they were seized.

Mapp was arrested and charged under Ohio Statue 2905.34 for possession of obscene material. "No person shall knowingly have in his possession or under his control an obscene, lewd, or lascivious book, print, or picture. Whoever violates this section shall be fined not less than $200 nor more than

---

[15]   State's motion to dismiss before the Supreme Court of United States, p. 5.

$2,000 or imprisoned of less than one nor more than seven years, or both." Mapp was sentenced from one to seven years in the Ohio State Women's Reformatory and received bail for $2,500.

The supplemental brief for the state of Ohio states on page 9 that

> The Record establishes that there was no misconduct on the part of the police in securing the evidence. The incident which took place between the appellant and the police prior to the search was brought about through no fault of the police. By her conduct, the appellant provoked the situation which made it necessary for the police to handcuff her if a peaceable search was to be conducted.[16]

Yet even the *Cleveland Plain Dealer* called the search of Mapp's house a three-hour siege. On May 24, 1957, the front page of the paper screamed: "Policy House Closed After 3-Hour Siege." The accompanying picture was of Carl Delau kneeling near a trunk full of California Gold Policy. To the reader it would seem Dollree Mapp was caught red handed.

---

[16]   Supplemental Brief, State of Ohio, p. 9.

CHAPTER THREE
Carl Delau and Dollree Mapp

I never met the great ballplayer, but Carl Delau somehow reminds me of Joe DiMaggio. At eighty-four he is tall, lean, well dressed and very dapper. His hair is now a silvery gray, and with his beautiful tweed jacket and camel-colored slacks he exudes the aura of a retired professional, a person of success. He looks like a man of leisure—confident, elegant. He reminds me of "old Hollywood," his hair combed back, his outdoorsy clothing, from his polo socks and loafers to his beautiful sports coats. His home and his dress are immaculate: first class, all the way. The *Cleveland Plain Dealer* referred to him as "the handsome, 6 foot three policeman who..." and then went on to tell the tale of Delau's latest crime fighting foray.[1]

Despite this sophisticated and genteel appearance, one finds on the inside a simpler man, not flashy and not drawn to the limelight. In that respect he was the opposite of Dollree Mapp. She was eye-catching, voluptuous, and a bit on the shady side: he was honest and hardworking. Gregarious and social, he was easy to get along with and easy to work for. He gained the respect of others and was clearly well liked. He could, and still can, spin a great yarn, and being with him transports you back to a different era.

Today he spends his time as president of the prestigious Beaver Creek Club, a private club for hunting enthusiasts in Cleveland. He serves as president at the pleasure of the membership, and is now in his fourteenth year. The job furthers his image, creating the opportunity for the retired police officer to look like an outdoors man featured in the Orvis or L. L. Bean catalogs. Carl Delau

---

[1] *Cleveland Plain Dealer*, May 20, 1959.

once resided at 1063 Cove Avenue in Lakewood, Ohio. Today he lives in the country in Novelty, Ohio, on the outskirts of Cleveland proper. His white A-frame house stands proudly on several acres, giving the retired police officer and his dogs privacy and a comfortable life. Passionate about hunting and dogs, he owns three hunting canines and has lovingly built kennels for them. His day is as neat and organized as his home. He rises early, runs his dogs, eats breakfast, and reads the local paper for about an hour before going on with his day.

A profile of Carl Delau in the *Cleveland Plain Dealer* once characterized him as a man who lives police work twenty-four hours a day. He is a bachelor, clearly by choice. He never married, probably because he never made the time. The job was consuming. What spare time he had went to his hobby, skeet and trap shooting. Delau was and is an expert marksman. When he wasn't chasing criminals, he was hunting pheasants and other game birds.

The man who became Dollree Mapp's chief nemesis began life as Carl Irvin Delau. His parents, born in Poland of German nationals, emigrated from Lotz, Poland, to the United States in May of 1913. His mother came from a large clan named Lehman. In contrast, his father was an orphan. The two traveled through Ellis Island, New York, with the first two of their eight children, girls ages three and one, to Cleveland. On the advice of others, Mr. Delau changed his name, dropping or adding parts, his son does not know. But in an attempt to "Americanize" his name, perhaps he made it more complicated. Pronounced DAY-louw, it is easily mispronounced as well as misspelled. The young family quietly established a home on the west side of Cleveland, following several family members to that Midwestern city from Europe. Carl Delau was the fifth child, born August 6, 1918, in Cleveland.[2]

---

[2]   Today his sister, now ninety-one, resides in a nursing home. Another sister is eighty-nine, a brother who would be eighty-seven has passed away along with several other siblings, and his remaining brother is seventy-eight.

Their roots were German and the neighborhood was a haven for those that had emigrated from Germany. The Delaus spoke more German than English in their west side home. With a carpenter father and a homemaker mother, Carl Delau's most vivid childhood memories were ones of hard work and frugality. His teenage years witnessed the Great Depression. Despite his skill as a qualified carpenter, Mr. Delau had trouble remaining employed. Consequently, Carl and many of his siblings worked jobs after school and during the summer to help support the family. From the time he was fifteen until his eighteenth birthday, Carl Delau worked during the summer for a greenhouse truck farmer six days a week, ten hours a day. During the school year he worked each Saturday.

His parents were Protestants who attended church services held in German. His father's one pleasure outside of his job was to sing in the church choir, of course in German. His mother, quiet and steady, made sure that her children were sent to school with clean clothes and a packed lunch. The family tenets of hard work, honesty, and faith were ingrained at an early age. Carl said to me: "My youth was not all that impressive. It was one of hard work during the Depression, one of eight children of German parents who emphasized hard work, honesty, and religion over schooling, but I am not finding fault with this."[3]

Education was viewed as less vital to success and not significant since neither of Delau's parents had much in the way of formal schooling. Of all the Delau children, only one obtained college credit, a brother who attended college in 1947 after returning home from World War II. The potential was there. Carl Delau describes his older brother as the "brains of the family." He graduated high school a year early. He mastered the Gregg system of short-hand, which facilitated a job as a court stenographer. This allowed him to spend two years at Ohio State, where he excelled at language studies. Despite his

---

[3]   Letter from Carl Delau dated June 7, 2001.

academic skills, full time employment and no financial assistance proved too much and he never received a degree.

Carl Delau classifies himself as "a bad scholar." While his mental acuity leaves this in doubt, it is clear from discussions with him that his interest in "book learning" was minimal. He attended West Technical High School in Cleveland and graduated in January 1937. The only courses he enjoyed were history and shop. He quickly found employment as a mechanical draftsman apprentice at a steel wire manufacturing company. Although a long way from his future career as a police officer, he claimed that "working with machines and tools assisted me when I was called into federal service,"[4] meaning the military. Delau had proudly enrolled in the Ohio National Guard after high school and served throughout his four years as an apprentice. But things changed on March 5, 1941, when his unit was called to active duty.

Carl Delau entered the United States Army as part of the 107th Calvary. This was a good assignment. It allowed him to serve with friends and the prestige of the 107th was such that it commanded respect. Meanwhile, labor unions were organizing and turning his steel wire manufacturing firm into a union shop. While he was not against the union, the disruption and strong-arm tactics made leaving easier. On March 1, 1941, Carl Delau was called up for a one- year tour. Knowing it would be much longer, but assured that by having completed his apprenticeship he had a job to return to, he looked forward to serving in the renowned calvary unit.

"Perhaps being of German descent, there must have been a trace of militarism within me," Carl Delau wrote to me.[5] In fact I think the choice to serve was more straightforward. He contemplated service in one of the local national guard artillery batteries, engineering companies, and infantry regiments, but seeing a cavalry company on parade made his service selection easy. The teenager had witnessed the 107th Cavalry, Troops A and B, an all-

4.   Letter from Carl Delau dated September 2001.
5.   Ibid.

horse unit, which had combined with troops from other Ohio cities to form a regiment of horsemen in uniform. "This decided the issue for me," he recalled.[6]

The 107th Cavalry began as a private militia, comprised mostly of blue bloods from the Cleveland area who loved horses. The local group later became part of the Ohio National Guard and served in 1917 in World War I. In 1939 the 107th was filled, and only those with social connections stood a chance of filling any vacancy. However, World War II changed that.

Whereas the capacity was 60 men per troop unit, the numbers quickly swelled to 115 per troop unit. Delau, who upon his initial inquiry was told that the unit was full, was called up. "But alas, instead of becoming a horse soldier, our horses were taken away from our troops and given to units in other cities of the 107th while we became a mechanized troop and squadron."[7] The horses were gone, but arriving at Camp Forest, Tennessee, in March of 1941, he found the latest equipment available, even better than what most regular army units had.

Delau's training began in earnest. He had only owned a twenty-two caliber rifle and had no firearms training of any kind. His machinist skills facilitated his training as an armorer, and quickly he was made responsible for forty-eight water-cooled thirty-caliber machine guns; twenty-four fifty-caliber machine guns, and many other firearms such as forty-five-caliber automatics, rifles, and Thompson machine guns. At the rank of private first class, he was introduced to what would become his hobby and lifelong passion.

Delau continued to train at Camp Forest until December 7, 1941. Carl Delau recalls where he was on the fateful day, as most everyone of his generation can do. "On December 7, Sunday, with half of the regiment away on pass, all were ordered back to camp and by night fall, we were alerted with the orders that we were to move to the west coast. By the time trains were obtained and the week it took us to get to Fort Ord, it was Christmas time. Once

---

6   Ibid.

7   Ibid.

we got to California we gained the information that our destination was to have been the Philippines but due to the shortage of boats, both battle and transports, we stayed in California performing coastal defense duties."[8] Delau was promoted to sergeant, and soon after, platoon sergeant.

By March 1943 Delau was off to Fort Riley, Kansas, to attend Cavalry Officer Candidate School. Ninety days later, with little trouble, he was commissioned a second lieutenant in the United States Army at the age of twenty-five. He was top in the class in the knowledge and use of weapons. He was physically fit. "Only one class mate could outrun me," he said.[9]

Again, the path traveled before proved so beneficial, according to Carl Delau. His previous stint as an armorer led him to become an instructor in the weapons department at Fort Riley. A great assignment, good quarters, "working with firearms, my love,"[10] and the Officer's Club nearby, Delau could ask for little more. However, with a war on, at his own request, he was transferred to the 3rd Cavalry by year's end.

Delau was assigned to E Troop in an assault gun troop of the 3rd Cavalry. He spent a month in England training on new equipment and shortly thereafter went to France. In the first week of August 1944 he began serving with the 3rd Army under General George Patton. His unit saw a great deal of action, fighting in France, Germany, and Austria. Shortly before the war ended, his unit came upon a slave labor camp in Ebensee, Austria, that housed 14,000 persons of all nationalities, some Jewish, yet no prisoners of war. It was a sight he would never forget.

On October 17, 1944, his commander, a lieutenant colonel, along with the squadron executive officer and a major approached Delau. He said to him, "Delau, let's take a run down to the Mozelle and scout out a river crossing site." Delau recalls the rest:

---

8   Letter from Carl Delau dated October 2001.
9   Ibid.
10   Ibid.

October 1944 was a very wet month during which time we were in our fox holes, out
posting along the Mozelle River while an infantry division was working hard and
suffering in an attempt to take the forts of Metz. Parking our Jeep in the woods, we
were in and out of various locations when we apparently ventured just a little to far out
in the open when a machine gun from the opposite side, then a second gun opened up
and struck me in the arm and entered the chest. This is how a person earns a Purple
Heart.[11]

After surgery in France and a period of recuperation in England, Carl Delau
rejoined his same unit now in Germany on December 26, 1944, a cold, wintry
day. He remained there and in Austria until the war in Europe ended. The 3rd
Cavalry was ordered back to France for return to the United States. However,
his unit was being sent to China for the big push against the Japanese. "It was
just as we reported back to camp that the bomb was dropped. After this,
everyone wanted to be discharged and head for home."[12] When the war ended
in May, the 3rd Cavalry celebrated its ninety-ninth birthday on May 19, 1945.
Patton himself had once commanded the 3rd in the 1930s and attended the
festivities.

After five years of being away from home, Carl Delau decided to leave the
army. He was offered a chance to stay with the 3rd since he had acted as troop
commander and was promised a promotion to captain. He decided against it but
remained at Fort Bragg, North Carolina, until late November 1945 to help
discharge troops.

His love for the 3rd Cavalry remains strong more than fifty years later. The
present 3rd is located at Fort Carson, Colorado. A unit of 5,200 strong, it is
well armed, so much so that the weight of their tanks and artillery prevent any
quick deployment outside the United States. The current officers of the 3rd
continue to invite the World War II veterans, despite their dwindling numbers,
for events. And the 3rd still has reunions, always attended by Carl Delau, who

---

[11]   Ibid.

[12]   Ibid.

serves on the board of the 3rd Cavalry Association. His army years were a time of great growth for him, in confidence, and emerging skills such as leadership and in increasing knowledge of firearms. The boy who had left home returned as a young man with a sense of purpose but little direction.

When Carl Delau left the Army in late November 1945 he was unsure where to go. The GI Bill made a college education available, yet at twenty-seven Delau "felt too old to cut it with a much younger crowd."[13] He felt that factory work or office work would be too mundane. Although no one in his family had ever been a police officer, Delau turned to this work because of the similarity it had to the military. Delau's entry into law enforcement was typical of the day. Leadership, firearms training, and thinking on your feet were all skills acquired in military service and were easily transferred to police work.

He had gained much from his military service including leadership, astute skills, and the ability to manage people. These led him to consider a career in law enforcement, although getting on the city payroll was not as easy as he thought. No one from his family had engaged in police work. "In fact, until I joined, I believe no one in our family had ever been in a court room or police station."[14] Of course he was forgetting his court stenographer brother, but the fact was that policing was not a familiar occupation.

In November 1945 Carl Delau read a notice in the *Cleveland Plain Dealer* that the city was hiring part-time police officers. The department had seen its staff diminish during the war and by December of 1945 was looking for some part time staff. Delau recounts the story of his entry onto the force. He went to see the director of public safety in City Hall, only to be told that the city was not hiring and he should come back next year when a notice for the civil service exam was posted in the newspaper. Knowing that the man was lying, Delau returned the next day completely in uniform "boots, britches, and all."[15]

---

[13]   Letter from Carl Delau dated June 2001.

[14]   Ibid.

[15]   Ibid.

The same gentleman told Delau again that the city was not hiring and the director of public safety was not available. Delau told him, "I'll wait." Shortly thereafter, a kind clerk ushered him into see the assistant director of public safety. After a brief interview and the completion of bureaucratic forms, Carl Delau was told to return January 1, 1946, to begin service as a temporary police officer. Thirty officers were sworn in with him on January 2, 1946.

Cleveland had found its quality of life greatly diminished during the war years. Crime was up and enforcement was down. The time was ripe for reform and Delau was part of that movement. He was quickly considered for full-time employment. In the spring of 1946 he sat for the civil service examination with some 1,800 men. By July 16, 1946,he was sworn in as a Cleveland police officer. So busy was the academy that he did not attend the training school until the summer of 1948. Postwar Cleveland was intent on reversing the downslope of the previous years.

After only two weeks of training Delau was assigned to the Accident Investigation Program (AIU). Such a staffing problem existed, few officers had uniforms, so Delau was permitted to work in civilian clothes, assigned to what was known as the Hit-Skip Unit, today more commonly known as hit and run investigations today.[16] When he finally did attend the police academy, Delau graduated in one of the top positions in his class and was assigned again to the Accident Investigation Unit. This was a prestigious assignment, and now in uniform, Delau worked the 11 P.M. to 7 A.M. shift.

It was during this duty, as a young police officer, that he first encountered Shondor Birns. Delau would arrest Birns in the first of many meetings. No police officer on the Cleveland force would come to know Alex Birns better than Carl Delau. The two would become each other's nemesis, playing a cat and mouse game of the gangster versus cop.

---

[16]   Police Report of August 10, 1949, Cleveland Police Department. Provided by Carl Delau to the author.

At 2:30 A.M. on August 9, 1949, Patrolman Carl Delau and his partner, Mike Vourliotou, caught a speeder. Parked on East 9th Street, the two were watching for traffic violations on Shore Drive. They noticed an auto coming off the Main Avenue bridge going east at a high rate of speed. Delau driving, they immediately set out after the car but did not overtake the car until 49th Street. Patrol Car 341 clocked the speeder at sixty-five miles per hour and noted that it had passed four cars on wet pavement. At one point the police car sped to seventy-five miles per hour to catch the 1949 Cadillac convertible coup, license number AB-373. The flashy automobile eventually pulled over, and Delau approached the car alone.

The young patrolman told the driver that he was clocked at sixty-five miles per hour. The driver agreed, stating that he was in a hurry to get home. When Delau asked for the drivers' license and he saw the name, it was clear that this was no ordinary driver and no ordinary traffic violation. The license read,"Al. Shondor Birns, 24631 Lakeshore." Birns was well known to all of Cleveland's police and certainly to an up-and-coming officer like Delau. Delau asked him how it was that he was heading home when the route he had just speedily taken was nowhere near his business on East 105th and the Hotel Hollenden, his current residence. The Lakeshore address was a summer residence he replied.

Delau then informed Birns of the city regulation that required that anyone operating a vehicle at more than sixty miles per hour be booked at the police station. Birns suggested that the ticket be written for fifty-five miles per hour, still a hefty fine for traveling so fast. Delau said no and gave instructions for Birns to turn his vehicle around and follow him to the station. Birns then remarked, "Can't we get together and talk this thing over," to which Delau replied, "No."[17] Birns followed Delau to the station, went to the booking window and proceeded with the arrest.

Since Birns was by far the most notable of Cleveland's bad guys, the *Cleveland Plain Dealer* reported the story with a twist; that Birns had

---

[17]   Ibid.

attempted to bribe Delau and the straight-arrow officer refused to yield to temptation. The headlines read: "Speeder Birns Jailed, Finds He Can't Buy Cop."[18] The article lead stated, "Patrolman Carl Delau, unawed by underworld influence and not tempted by its wealth, put Alex Shondor Birns in jail for speeding today."[19] The press noted that the exchange included comments by Birns such as "Don't you know who I am?" When Delau smiled and nodded the affirmative, Birns says "Let's not be silly. Let's make a deal,"and pulled out his billfold.

Delau, they report, replied as his voice went hard, "Put that billfold back. With your reputation, you're the last guy in the world I'd take anything from, even if I was on the take which I'm not."

Birns then replied, "Listen, I'm one guy you can take it from and trust. I wouldn't jam you up." "Follow me in," replied Delau curtly.[20]

This exchange sounds dramatic but did not happen. Delau's police report clearly states that the only violation that Birns was guilty of was speeding and that "at no time while in the company of Al Birns was there any remarks of giving a bribe or the request of excepting (accepting) one. If there was an inference of one it wasn't noticed at the time spent in conversation. At the time that we stopped him was but a matter of a few minutes during which time I told him that he had to be booked at the station."[21] Birns was arrested on Traffic Violation 2407, charged at Central Booking Station. He paid the fifty-dollar fine and court cost before Judge Perry B. Jackson.

Years later, Delau is consistent in stating that there was no attempt to bribe him by Birns. Still, the story was good reading for the *Plain Dealer*. Even the most rudimentary of Birns's moves was reported. Hungry for a story, the press made something out of the encounter. It was the first meeting between Delau

---

18   *Cleveland Plain Dealer*, August 11, 1949. Provided to the author by Carl Delau.

19   Ibid.

20   Ibid.

21   Police Report, Cleveland Police Department, August 10, 1949, Arrest report of Shondor Birns.

and Birns and was much less inauspicious than was reported. But not all their meetings would be so mundane. The encounter did afford each the ability to size the other up. As Delau became a leader in combating the vice activities in Cleveland, Birns would be forced to consider how best to deal with the clever and younger police officer.

~~~

Dollree Mapp, too, came from humble beginnings, yet there the similarities end. Now an older woman, a grandmother, she has not lost the sparkle and feistiness of her youth. She has a flare for the dramatic and a salty vocabulary designed to shock more so than communicate. I found her coy and cagey, enjoying the repartee with me. She served time in prison for drug possession in the 1970s, and despite the fact that fame comes from her transgressions with the law, she warms to the attention that intermittently comes her way. While the legal tangle with Delau made her famous (or rather infamous), she relishes the spotlight and graces it with colorful tales, embellished with curse words and opinionated bravado.[22] She could be forthcoming and standoffish, funny and combative. I liked her but was wary of her.

Born to a white school teacher, she was one of seven children. Dollree revealed little about her father, named Sam, other than he was overbearing. She was raised in a strict household. At about age ten, she decided to run away from home and hitchhiked over two hundred miles to her Aunt Dora's. Her aunt eventually called her parents to inform them of their daughter's whereabouts and upon her return Dollree experienced a severe beating. She recounted the story, telling me that she was almost bleeding from the severity of her father's hand. At sixteen she became pregnant. Refusing to give up the child, her father

---

[22]   Her broken promises to meet with me were frequently met with excuses and evasiveness. Finally, after speaking with me numerous times by telephone she agreed to see me. It seemed to be a test of my fortitude more than a scheduling conflict.

threw Dollree out of the house for disgracing the family. When the infant Barbara was born, Dollree refused to put her up for adoption and turned to an old friend, Jimmy Bivens, for money and a place to stay. She would later marry him, but the marriage would prove as violent as her childhood and would eventually end in divorce.

Dollree finished high school and dreamed of going to New York to work on Broadway or in the fashion industry. Early photographs of her show a beautiful woman, sensuous and full of life. She always appeared in her finery, dressing with flair and sex appeal. These attributes did not carry her onto the stage but instead were her entree into particular social circles in Cleveland. Her striking looks brought her attention from wealthy and powerful men, both white and black, upstanding and shady. These same men who brought her opportunity were ultimately her downfall. Whether it was the lack of opportunity or the ease with which men were drawn to her, Dollree Mapp would experience both the highs and lows of her life in terms of men.

At the time of the bombing of Donald King's home, Dollree Mapp knew everyone involved: the police, the suspects, the witnesses, even the judge. She became the focal point of the story, not just because she challenged her treatment by the police, but she had connected the dots for each of the principals. She knew Donald King well and at times carried bets and payoffs for him in the policy house. Virgil Ogletree, the bombing suspect that brought the police to 14705 Milverton Road, was a friend of Dollree's and remains so to this day. Mapp claimed that Virgil was in the lower apartment the entire time the search of Mapp's residence took place. She quipped that she did not believe Virgil was involved in the bombing because he was so mousy. And of course she was familiar with Officers Michael Haney and Carl Delau.

Several days before the bombing of King's home, Mapp was supposed to go to the movies with Edward Keeling. Keeling was kind to Dollree and good to her daughter Barbara. She claimed that they never married because Keeling was already married at the time. (A minor detail for Mapp though a much larger, even insurmountable stumbling block for most.) Instead of taking her to the movies, Keeling called and cancelled. When pressed by Dollree why he was unable to keep their date, he provided her with no explanation. It was only later that she understood what happened that evening. Edward Keeling was arrested and jailed for his involvement in the bombing of King's house, and when Mapp visited him in jail, Keeling suggested to her that the reason he broke their date should be clear to her. He encouraged her to provide him with an alibi by telling the police that he was at home at the time of the bombing.

Even Mapp's impending legal woes were financed by a man impressed with her worldliness and beauty. Introduced to a wealthy white businessman, Mapp caught his eye and kept him interested with her wit. Under the pretext of needing a premium, this insurance salesman would eventually be convinced by Dollree Mapp to pay her legal fees she owed to A. L. Kearns and Walter Green. It is doubtful that Dollree Mapp would have pursued litigation so vigorously without the funding and generosity of her male benefactor.[23]

But not all her relationships were profitable. She described her first husband, Bivens, as "a bastard and a brute."[24] Their marriage was volatile and the intensity of the attraction was matched by the intensity of the incompatibility. She recounted a day when Bivens put a gun to her chest and pulled back the trigger as if to shoot her. She told him boldly that she did not believe he would do it, but the incident left her shaken and weary. Bivens, too, had his fill. A professional boxer, he claimed in their divorce proceedings that Mapp was trying to kill him, or at least ruin his career, by feeding him fatty foods such as fried chicken.

Dollree Mapp was smart and street savvy and it took her no time to connect most of the events. She showed this on October 9, 1957, at 6:32 P.M. when she went to the office of John T. Corrigan, the prosecutor, and made a statement before Corrigan, Delau, and Haney about the bombing of Donald King's house.

---

[23]   I asked Ms. Mapp to reveal the name of the individual. She refused.

[24]   Interview with Dollree Mapp by the author, March 15, 1993.

She told the police what she knew without a promise of anything in exchange. Why she came forward is unclear. Perhaps it was to save her own neck or perhaps to cut a deal at some point. She was dating Keeling at the time of the bombing and she assisted him with policy and clearing house, even running the California Gold and International Houses out of her own home. She talked with Shondor Birns regularly when he would call for Keeling. Just as Delau and Haney suspected, Dollree Mapp was intimately involved in the numbers and policy games of chance.

She was aware that people were paying $200 per week to Shon (as she called him) to keep the peace, and she knew that some were unhappy with Donald King because he refused to abide by this peacekeeping arrangement. Keeling told Dolly that someone would "straighten King out" someday. She was aware that King would be made to cooperate or would be put into line in some way. The bombing came as no surprise then, and the concern for an alibi by Keeling further supported her suspicion of why and by whom King's home was firebombed.

Mapp continued to fill in the blanks, keeping Haney, Delau, and Corrigan mesmerized by the details and knowledge she had of events. Much of what she said they could confirm through other sources. She provided them with details that were both original and credible. She recounted that Shondor Birns had traveled to Florida at one point to "let things cool off." She knew this because she took a collect telephone call from Birns to Keeling at her house. Birns gave her his motel number and chatted with her. Their banter was light, Mapp asking Birns to bring her back something. Later Mapp received a nice gift with a card that said, "From your greatest friend, Shon."

But Birns clearly expected some quid pro quo. When he found out later that Dollree went to Cooney's office for a talk, Birns called her and confronted her. She told Shon that the meeting had not taken place. Birns expressed hope that she wouldn't do such a thing and that she realized who her friends were. She inquired where he heard such a thing about her talking to the police and he revealed only that he had "friends." Birns had more than friends. He had a network of cops, clerks, reporters, judges, and others around the courtroom whom he paid off in return for information. The threat was subtle but it was nevertheless hard to miss.

Corrigan and Haney and Delau realized that Mapp's knowledge of the events before and after the King bombing were so valuable that Dollree was offered to testify. The three-page-single spaced statement was signed and dated by both her and the police and states that she was getting nothing in exchange for her court appearance. Dollree made her statement after regular business hours so that it was unlikely that anyone would know that she had talked to the police.[25] It must have taken her at least an hour to tell this story. She made plans to testify in court as to what she knew but later decided against it. While it was never given as the exact reason, clearly Birns's pressure contributed to her change of heart.

Dollree had good reason to fear Birns. Once when Mervyn Gold was planning to snitch on Shon to the FBI, Birns found out about it. Birns was at the Theatrical Club, a posh nightclub, when he took a short telephone call. He left abruptly and was gone about an hour. Later the police found Gold dead—beaten up and dumped after a rough ride in the trunk of a car. When they investigated and searched the car, it appeared as though the perpetrator had slammed his or her hand in the trunk latch mechanism. Not surprisingly, when Birns appeared back at the Theatrical Club, his hand and thumb were swollen and bloody.

---

[25]   Officer Haney had the only copy of this secret meeting, and he showed it to the author.

CHAPTER FOUR
The Fourth Amendment

In little more than fifty words the United States Constitution outlaws unreasonable searches and seizures:

> The right of the people to be secure in their persons, houses, papers, and effects, against unreasonable searches and seizure, shall not be violated, and no warrants shall issue, but upon probable cause, supported by oath or affirmation, and particularly describing the place to be searched, and the persons or things to be seized.

This, the Fourth Amendment, like so many other provisions of the Bill of Rights, was aimed at a specific, historical grievance.

The events of the thirty years prior to the writing and passage of the Fourth Amendment are highly significant in elevating the principle of search and seizure to a constitutional right in American jurisprudence rather than continuing merely as legal principle. The use of the general warrant by the British antagonized the colonists and was central to the eventual break by the colonies from the mother country. However, laws regulating search and seizure long preceded the decades before 1791. Throughout the long history of search and seizure law, the dominant theme is that "a man's house is his castle."[1]

A right to be left alone in one's own home is universally recognized in the earliest of legal codes.[2] In ancient times, breaking into another's house at night

---

[1]   Nelson B. Lasson, *The History and Development of the Fourth Amendment to the United States Constitution* (Baltimore: Johns Hopkins University Press, 1937), p. 13.

[2]   In addition, several citations in the Bible support the theme of the sanctity of one's home. See Josh. 7:10–26; Josh. 2:1–7; Gen. 19:4–11; Deut. 24:10.

could result in the death penalty.[3] Roman law clearly delineates the right against search and seizure. Cicero said that one's home was a place of refuge sacred for all men, despite the fact that searches at the time were very general and the authority to search was virtually unlimited. The searches, however, were broader than the seizures.[4] The origin of the famous maxim, "Every man's house is his castle," often credited to the English Lord Coke, is not an original English principle but one borrowed from the Romans. "Nemo de domo sua extrahi debet."[5] Anglo-Saxon law reflects this Roman law influence.

Search and seizure law began to develop in England in the first half of the fourteenth century and was dominated by disdain for the *general warrant*. These legal documents were issued by the ruling monarch and were valid for the duration of his or her lifetime. It was not uncommon to arrest all suspected of having committed a certain type of crime and imprison them until further orders by the king. The result of this general inquisition was a rather long imprisonment, two to three years not being out of the ordinary.[6] Objections to the Crown's methods of search and seizure were made, particularly by printers, those accused of libel and sedition, and by merchants and others who were coerced by search and seizure to obey the tax laws.

Until about the seventeenth century, the Crown had unrestricted power in the use of search and seizure. An early example of this took place in 1335 when innkeepers in English port cities were ordered to search their guests for counterfeit monies. If an innkeeper discovered that a guest had entered the country with false currency, he was allowed to keep one fourth of it. However, official searches were conducted to check up on the innkeeper in order to ensure that he was carrying out his function under the act. The employees of

---

[3]   See Article 21 of the Code of Hammurabi in W. W. Davies, *Code of Hammurabi and Moses* (Cincinnati: Kessinger Publishing, 1915), p. 33.

[4]   Lasson, *History and Development of the Fourth Amendment*, p. 15.

[5]   Ibid., p. 15.

[6]   Ibid., p. 22.

the Crown were in turn allowed to keep a quarter of any false monies found.[7]

The use or search and seizure was expanded significantly during the Elizabethan and Stuart eras, which were known for suppression of the printed word, religion, treason, and seditious libel. Laws passed in this period were longstanding in significance; this is the beginning of the frequent use of search and seizure to curtail the rights of free press and free speech. By 1557 the Tudor licensing system had passed an act to implement the Stationers' Company. Power was granted to this company to "make search whenever it shall please them in any place, shop house, chamber, or building or any printer, binder, or book seller whatever within our Kingdom of England."[8] The Company's power was expanded in 1566 by the first act of the Court of Star Chamber, which licenced books, placed restrictions upon printing, and the like. In 1586 this power was reaffirmed by the Star Chamber, which stiffened the penalties and the degree of censorship. The act also expanded the use of search and seizure to keep rebellious writers and printers in check. The use of search and seizure by way of the Stationers' Company was also responsible for the suppression of both Catholic and Puritan dissenting literature under the Tudor reign.

Warrants during this period were not specific; no person was necessarily specified, nor place. No oath was necessary to secure a warrant before a magistrate and no probable cause was required. The breadth of a search and the seizure that followed were determined by the holder of the warrant. In sum, the searching agent had free rein in carrying out his task.[9]

---

[7]   Telford Taylor, *Two Studies in Constitutional Interpretation* (Columbus: Ohio State University Press, 1969), p. 25.

[8]   *Marcus v. Search Warrants at Property at 104 E. 10th Street, Kansas City, Missouri*, 367 U.S. 717, 728 (1961).

[9]   A warrant such as this was issued in 1593 for libelous acts concerning posters. This led to the arrest of one Thomas Kidd, whose seized papers revealed a relationship with Christopher Marlowe. Marlowe's atheism was then explored by the Privy Council. Marlowe was killed in a tavern brawl.

Each regime in the seventeenth century used search and seizure to suppress publication. During the reign of James I (1603-1625), the Crown began to use another device to carry out searches: the writ or warrant of assistance. These were general search warrants, probably created by statute in 1662.[10] These writs, or warrants, derived their name from commanding all officers and subjects of the Crown "to assist" in their execution.[11] Some of the warrants and writs were worded very broadly; some were more specific. Charles I (1625-1649) used the general warrant and the writ of assistance against those who had spoken out against his attempt to collect a tonnage and poundage duty.

The general warrant and the writ of assistance were used frequently to enforce sedition laws. In 1637 the Star Chamber permitted censorship that was even more strict, and gave approval to search for seditious persons or papers, day or night.[12] One notable victim of this was Sir Edward Coke, an authority on the common law but more importantly, an opponent of the Crown. The Privy Council sent men to search him for seditious papers as he lay on his deathbed. Virtually all his writings, jewelry, money, and his will were seized by the authority of a general warrant. His chambers at Inner Temple were also ransacked. It took his heirs seven years to recover any of Coke's belongings, and his will was never returned.[13]

Attempts at reform were made. In 1640, during the Reformation, the Star Chamber was abolished, as was the Court of High Commission. However, the Privy Council still functioned, examining evidence and committing persons to jail. By 1641 the House of Commons resolved that the search for papers of members of Parliament was a breach of privilege. However, Parliament soon forgot the indiscretions of preceding regimes and by 1643 an act was passed that regulated printing. The Act contained a severe censorship provision

---

[10] Taylor, *Two Studies*, p. 28.

[11] Lasson, *History and Development of the Fourth Amendment*, pp. 53-54.

[12] Prior to this, warrants were only executed during daylight hours.

[13] Lasson, *History and Development of the Fourth Amendment*, pp. 31-32.

allowing agents of the Crown a broad power to search. This Act of 1643 motivated Milton to write *Areopagitica*, urging for a free press.[14]

During this time British citizens became the victims of another type of tax, the excise, giving rise to a hint of widespread intolerance of search and seizure laws. The excise tax was used to subsidize the war effort, and with it came an unlimited authority to invade the privacy of homes to search for "unaccustomed goods." The excise tax became closely identified with the practice of search and seizure. Its denunciation gave rise to the development of common law on seizure of persons and property by the government.[15]

About this time, a treatise by Chief Justice Hale was published relating the history of pleas of the Crown. Contained in this work, *History of the Pleas of the Crown*, were several recommendations that crudely resembled the language of the future Fourth Amendment of the U.S. Constitution. For instance, the party asking for a warrant was to be examined under oath and made to give the reasons for suspecting some person or persons of a crime. This seems to be a forerunner of the probable cause requirement. Furthermore, Hale recommended that a warrant specify the name and description of the person or persons to be arrested. The warrant must not be written in general terms or be left blank for the searcher to complete later.[16]

Many felt that Parliament would heed Hale's commentary and limit the scope of the general warrant, but his treatise was of little influence. Parliament instead passed a new Licencing Act to regulate the press. Section 15 of the act contained a search and seizure provision.[17] The renewal of this act, however, was not effected by Parliament, but by a group of judges. One of these judges was later impeached for his participation. The Article of Impeachment contained one charge of issuing general warrants.[18] The lack of legislation

---

[14]   Ibid., pp. 32-33.

[15]   Taylor, *Two Studies*, p. 26.

[16]   Lasson, *History and Development of the Fourth Amendment*, p. 35.

[17]   Ibid., p. 38.

[18]   Ibid., p. 40.

granting the broad general searches, now being guaranteed by judges, fueled the growing intolerance for searches and seizures carried out by the Crown.

The intolerance with the heavy-handed use of search and seizure reached the high-water mark during 1762 in the events leading up to the famous cases of *Wilkes v. Wood*[19] and *Entick v. Carrington*.[20] John Wilkes, a member of Parliament, anonymously published a series of essays in 1762 entitled *North Briton*. Critical of the government, Number 45 was a particularly scathing attack on the latest speech of the king, hence a warrant was issued to arrest and seize the papers of the author of Number 45. The warrant was not specific as to the persons to be seized nor the place, and no probable cause was given. It was "a discretionary power given to messengers to search wherever their suspicions may chance to fall."[21] Over the course of three days, forty-nine persons were arrested. Finally, the actual printer of the *North Briton* was arrested, and Wilkes was revealed to be the author. All his private papers were seized. Wilkes was taken to the Tower of London but was released a few days later on the grounds of habeas corpus by reason of his privilege as a member of Parliament.[22]

All the jailed printers sued the government for false imprisonment.[23] Chief Justice Pratt declared the general warrant illegal, stating that in order for them to be valid, it needed to be specific as to the person and place to be searched. Wilkes then sued Woods,[24] the undersecretary who had witnessed the execution of the general warrant upon him. Chief Justice Pratt declared the general warrant contrary to common law, lacking probable cause and specificity. The jury

---

[19]   State Trials, XIX, 1029 (1765).

[20]   98 Eng. Rep. 489 (1763).

[21]   *Marcus v. Search Warrants at Property at 104 E. 10th Street, Kansas City, Missouri*, 367 U.S. 717, 728 (1961).

[22]   Lasson, *History and Development of the Fourth Amendment*, pp. 43-44.

[23]   *Huckle v. Money*, 95 Eng. Rep. 768 (1763).

[24]   *Wilkes v. Wood*, 98 Eng. Rep. 489 (1763).

awarded the particular plaintiffs damages of 300 pounds and the other plaintiff 200 pounds. Wilkes himself won a judgment of 1,000 pounds.[25]

"Wilkes and Liberty!" became a popular saying, and the ruling was praised by Englishmen as well as some colonists, who were also being subjected to the English general warrants. Wilkes became a familiar figure and began to correspond with some colonial leaders such as Samuel Adams, James Otis, John Hancock, and John Adams.[26] Justice Pratt was lauded and was later elevated to Lord Chancellor.

However, the general warrant was not yet banished from practice. In November of 1762 Lord Halifax issued a general warrant to search John Entick, the author of the *Monitor or British Freeholder*. The warrant was specific as to the person to be searched, but was vague as to what papers were to be seized or where the search was to take place. Entick's home was ransacked for four hours and a number of books and papers were seized.[27] Encouraged by the success of Wilkes, Entick sued and won.[28] Pratt, now Lord Camden, ruled on behalf of Entick that the messenger had made no inventory of what was seized, that no oath was given to support the search, that no probable cause was evident, and that the sweeping scope of the search lacked the specificity required by the common law. The warrant was declared invalid.

As a result of *Wilkes* and *Entick*, the House of Commons attempted to curtail the use of the general warrant. In February 1764 William Pitt tried to focus debate on the warrant, but discussion was postponed by government loyalists.

---

[25]   All told, the government in defending all actions arising from the warrant and the payment of judgments, spent approximately 100,000 British pounds. See Lasson, *History and Development of the Fourth Amendment*, pp. 41-45.

[26]   Ibid., pp. 45-46.

[27]   See this discussion in *Marcus v. Search Warrants at Property at 104 E. 10th Street, Kansas City, Missouri,* 367 U.S. 717, 728 (1961).

[28]   Entick v. Carrington, State Trials, XIX, 1029 (1765). The early members of the United States Supreme Court viewed this case as a landmark in search and seizure law. See *Boyd v. United States,* 116 U.S. 616 (1886).

Two years later, in April 1766, the House of Commons resolved that the use of general warrants in libel cases was illegal. However, a bill prohibiting the seizure of persons by general warrant was defeated. Finally the lower house passed a bill to restrain the use of the general warrant except in cases of treason or felony, but the House of Lords voted it down.[29]

General search warrants and writs of assistance were also used by the mother country against the colonists. In general, the British used these two legal maneuvers to regulate the importation of goods into the colonies to raise money and to protect English industry. For example, molasses was allowed to be imported into the colonies only if it came from the British West Indies. However, these British satellites couldn't produce enough molasses to meet the demands of the colonists, so France and Spain met the remainder of the demand, in obvious violation of the law. The British were unconcerned until the outbreak of the Seven Years War with France, when the colonists suddenly found the British strictly enforcing importation laws.[30] By 1761 the relationship between British customs houses and the colonists was tense, with custom officials using the writs of assistance and general warrants to search for smuggled goods.

In February 1761 all the writs of assistance expired due to the death of King George II. Sixty-three Boston merchants quickly petitioned the Courts of Massachusetts to address the validity of any new writs.[31] James Otis argued on behalf of the merchants, making an electrifying speech damning the use of general warrants.[32] John Adams, not yet a member of the bar and no more than twenty-five years of age, witnessed Otis's performance and marveled at his ideas. Fifty-seven years later, he recounted,

---

[29]   Lasson, *History and Development of the Fourth Amendment*, p. 49, n. 123.

[30]   Ibid., pp. 51-53.

[31]   Only Massachusetts and New Hampshire passed laws allowing writs of assistance or general warrants to be issued. Other colonies struggled with the issue but these were never culminated in law.

[32]   Taylor, *Two Studies*, pp. 36-37.

I do say in the most solemn manner, that Mr. Otis's oration against the Writs of Assistance once breathed into this nation the breath of Life. Then and there was the first scene of opposition to the arbitrage claims of Great Britain. Then and there the child Independence was born. In 15 years, namely, in 1776, he grew to manhood, and declared himself free.[33]

The significance of Otis's speech endured in the mind of Adams. During the Second Continental Congress he wrote to his wife Abigail,

When I look back to the year 1761 and recollect the argument concerning writs of assistance, in the superior court, which I have hitherto considered as the commencement of the controversy between Great Britain and America, and recollect the series of political events, the chain of causes to effects, I am surprised at the suddenness of this revolution.[34]

The events leading up to the Revolution occurred swiftly. The war with France was nearing an end, leaving Great Britain in dire need of funds. By 1763 England ordered that all laws should be more strictly enforced upon the colonists. In 1764 the Sugar Act was passed; in 1765 the infamous Stamp Act was enacted by Parliament. Riots broke out as a result.[35]

---

[33] *Works of John Adams*, X, 247-48, quoted in Lasson, *History and Development of the Fourth Amendment,* p. 59. Some argue that Adams's account of the events in the Courthouse are colored and imperfect. However, the significance of the event is undeniable. Frank P. Grinnell in "John Winthrop and the Constitutional Thinking of John Adams" says that he thinks Otis's impression on the young Adams could be Otis's most important contribution to American independence. See his article in *Massachusetts Historical Society Proceedings* (1929-1930), LXI I I, 98, 107, 115-16.

[34] Quoted in Mabel Hill, Liberty Documents, (New York, 1901), pp.188-89.

[35] Lasson, *History and Development of the Fourth Amendment*, pp. 68-69. An interesting attempt at using search and seizure to enforce the revenue raising laws was made in 1768 when John Hancock's boat "Liberty" was seized under a writ for landing Madeira wines without a duty payment. The crowd was angered by the violence of the seizure (his boat was anchored under the guns of a man-of-war in Boston Harbor) and the timing (it was near sunset). The boat was later forfeited in Admiralty Court and later bought by the Collector

The friction between the colonists and Great Britain was steadily growing. In 1772 a group of Bostonians appointed a committee of twenty-one individuals to state "the Rights of the Colonists."[36] James Otis, in his last known public act, presented the report of the committee. One of the "Infringements and Violations of Rights" was the searching powers of custom officials.[37]

The movement to codify the Rights of individuals swiftly followed the Boston Committee.[38] The colonists were intent on writing into their early state documents their rights, which they saw being jeopardized by the British choke hold. At least seven states incorporate some personal freedoms and liberties into

---

of Boston. Eventually it was used as a coast guard boat. However, in 1769, a mob, angry over the seizure of vessels based on unfounded suspicion, set the boat afire.

[36] Lasson, *History and Development of the Fourth Amendment*, p. 72, n. 74.

[37] Ibid., p. 72. A true test for the colonists concerning the use of search and seizure was to come. On August 28, 1777, the Continental Congress while in session, heard that a British army had landed. The Continental Congress recommended that all persons who had shown a distaste for the American cause, especially Quakers, be arrested and have their papers confiscated! These individuals were arrested and their homes were searched. They had no trial or hearing and were later sent off to Virginia. Known as the "Virginia Exiles" these first victims of American search and seizure, ironically Americans themselves, were returned to their homes in April of 1778 through the efforts of George Washington. See Ibid., pp. 76-77.

[38] Ironically, the Declaration of Independence is not considered by most scholars to be a precedent to the Fourth Amendment. The document was written to the king enumerating the grievances of the colonists. John Adams, who was one of the signers, revised Jefferson's draft but failed to include any mention of the intolerable uses of the general warrant. It is odd that the colonists passed up this opportunity to express their distaste for the egregious acts of the Crown by way of the general warrant. Some scholars disagree, inferring in the clause, "He has ...sent hither swarms of Officers to harass our people..." The outlawing of search and seizure by way or general warrants and writs or assistance. see Carl N. Becker, *Declaration of Independence* (New York, 1922), pp. 5ff. Also see Francis N. Thorpe, *Constitutional History of the United States* (Chicago, 1901), I I: 207, and Frederic J. Stimson, *Law of the Federal and State Constitutions of the United States* (Boston, 1908), p. 149, n. 10.

their constitutions.[39] The most notable of these for its similarity to the Fourth Amendment was the Virginia Bill of Rights written in 1776. Drafted by George Mason, who would later write portions of the Fourth Amendment, it was changed only slightly by James Madison.[40] The search and seizure provision, clause ten, read as follows:

> X. That general warrants whereby an officer or messenger may be commended to search suspected places without evidence of a fact committed or to seize any person or persons not named or whose offense is not particularly described and supported by evidence are grievous and oppressive and ought not to be granted.[41]

Note that the Virginia version focused solely on curtailing the general warrant.

After the Virginia Bill of Rights was drafted, a search and seizure provision was written into virtually every state's declaration or bill of rights. Pennsylvania included in its Declaration of Rights the oath requirement to support the granting of a warrant.[42] Massachusetts' Declaration of Rights of 1780, Article 14, included the phrase "unreasonable searches and seizures."[43]

---

[39]   Virginia, Pennsylvania, Maryland, North Carolina, Vermont, Massachusetts, and New Hampshire. The other six states either had no formal bill of rights or listed only a few. See Lasson, *History and Development of the Fourth Amendment*, p. 82.

[40]   Lasson, *History and Development of the Fourth Amendment*, p. 79.

[41]   Quoted in Benjamin P. Poore, *Federal and State Constitutions* (Washington: Government Printing Office, 1877), I, II: 1909.

[42]   "That the people have a right to hold themselves, their houses, papers, and possessions free from search and seizure, and therefore warrants without oaths or affirmation first made, affording a sufficient foundation for them, and whereby any officer or messenger may be commanded or required to search suspected places, or to seize any person or persons, his or their property, are contrary to that right, and ought not to be granted." Section 10. Quoted in Poore, Ibid., II: 1542.

[43]   "Every subject has a right to be secure from all unreasonable searches and seizures of his person, his house, his papers and his possessions. All warrants, therefore, are contrary to this right, if the cause or foundation of them be not previously supported by oath or affirmation, and if the order in the warrant to a civil officer, to make search in suspected places, or to arrest one or more suspected persons, or to seize their property, be not accompanied with

During the Constitutional Contention the search and seizure problem was swept up in the larger movement calling for a Bill of Rights. A codified list of liberties was not discussed until five days before the Convention was to adjourn. Elbridge Gerry, seconded by George Mason, moved for the preparation of a Bill of Rights. The motion failed. Edmund Randolph moved that the Constitution as drafted should not be sent to the states for ratification but should be reconsidered at another convention the following year when a Bill of Rights and other amendments could be properly debated and drafted in state conventions, and then added to the document. Despite support from Mason,[44] Randolph's motion failed. Mason, Gerry, and Randolph all refused to sign the Constitution.[45]

However, debate on the issue of a Bill of Rights reached such an impasse for the framers of the Constitution that it was unresolved as the process moved from Philadelphia to the state ratifying conventions. In Virginia, for example, lengthy debates took place over various liberties omitted in the Philadelphia document. Finally a committee was formed to prepare "recommended" amendments to be added to the Constitution soon after its adoption. This committee included Patrick Henry, George Wythe, John Marshall, Edmund Randolph, James Madison, and George Mason. Their fourteenth section dealt with the problem of unlimited searches and seizures.[46] Other states did much the same in their ratifying conventions, so that when the First Congress met in 1789, they had upwards of 200 proposed amendments from the states to consider.

---

a special designation of the person or objects of search, arrest, or seizure; and no warrant ought to be issued, but in cases, and with the formalities prescribed by the laws." It is clear that this provision was a forerunner of the Fourth Amendment. Again, note the thrust of the language; to curtail the abuses of the general warrant.

[44] George Mason refused to sign the Constitution because of the omission of a Bill of Rights. Of particular concern to him was a limitation upon the use of general warrants to search and seize.

[45] Catherine Drinker Bowen, *Miracle at Philadelphia* (Boston: Little, Brown, 1966: reprinted ed., 1986), pp. 244-53.

[46] Lasson, *History and Development of the Fourth Amendment*, p. 95.

When the First Congress met in June 1789 to draft a Bill of Rights, the immediate evil addressed by the Fourth Amendment[47] was the general warrant. The original Draft of the Amendment, as penned by James Madison, contained only one clause, and it concerned the warrant.

> The Rights of the people to be secured in their persons, their houses, their papers, and their other property, from all unreasonable searches and seizure, shall not be violated by warrants issued without probable cause, supported by oath or affirmation, or not particularly describing the places to be searched, or the persons or things to be seized.[48]

As it read, the intent of Madison's draft focused upon the warrant, not the search in and of itself. Madison and his Committee colleagues saw the warrant as the *authority* for unreasonable searches and seizures.[49] Eliminating its flagrant use was the solution the drafters envisioned.

The Committee of Eleven, composed of one member from each state, reported the provision as follows:

> The right of the people to be secured in their persons, houses, papers and effects shall not be violated by warrants issuing without probable cause, supported by oath or affirmation and not particularly describing the place to be searched, and the persons or things to be seized.[50]

Gerry corrected the mistake in phraseology to read, "The right of the people to be *secure* in their persons, houses, papers, and effects, *against unreasonable*

---

[47]   When drafted, the Fourth Amendment was the sixth numerically in the list of twelve amendments presented to the states for ratification. Of the twelve, only the last ten passed, thus the sixth numerically became the Fourth ratified. The Fourth Amendment as we know it was referred to as the Sixth Amendment in several early Supreme Court cases due to this historical fact. See *Ex Parte Burford*, 3 Cr. 448 2 L. Ed. 495 (1860) and *Ex Parte Bollman*, 8 U.S. (4 Cr.)75 (1807).

[48]   *Annals of Congress*, 1st Congress, 1st Session, p. 452 (1789).

[49]   Taylor, *Two Studies*, p. 41.

[50]   Lasson, *History and Development of the Fourth Amendment*, p. 101.

searches and seizures...." Congressman Benson of the Committee thought that Madison's phrase "by warrants issuing" was too weak. He move to strengthen it by substituting "and no warrant shall issue."[51] Benson's motion was rejected out of hand. If adopted, it would have had a distorting effect (as we shall see).

But then an incredible oversight of historical significance took place. On August 24th, a Committee of Three, made up of Benson, Sherman, and Sedgwick was formed, charged with the sole task of arranging the amendments in a logical order for final approval by Congress, and eventually the states. On his own "authority," it appears, *Benson reinstated his version which had previously been voted down* by the Committee of Eleven.[52] Seemingly no one noticed, and his handiwork, apparently never having been adopted by the House, became, after Senate and state approval, the Fourth Amendment.

Madison's draft proposal was clear and straightforward. It recognized and constitutionalized an old common law tradition; namely, a right of the people to be secure against *unreasonable* search and seizure. It went on to provide that this right "shall not be violated" *by general warrants.* This was a direct response to the crisis brought about by general warrants and writs of assistance in colonial America.

To guard against the generality abuse, Madison and the other framers provided that "...no Warrants shall issue, but upon probable cause, supported by Oath or affirmation [before a magistrate]." Moreover, any warrant that might be issued must particularly describe "the place to be searched, and the person or things to be seized." *It is noteworthy that nothing in Madison's proposal required the use of search warrants.* His declaration was purely negative: freedom from "unreasonable" intrusion shall not be violated by general warrants. Madison and the others focused upon the warrant, not the search in and of itself. They saw the general warrant as *authority* for unreasonable search and seizures. Thanks to

---

[51] *Annals of Congress*, 1st Congress, 1st Session, p. 783 (1789).

[52] Lasson, *History and Development of the Fourth Amendment*, p. 101. See also *House Journal*, August 24, 1789.

common law restrictions warrantless searches had never been a problem. All of the cases against which Otis railed were search warrant cases! That is true also of the great English landmark cases of the same ilk and era; namely, those involving Wilkes and Entick.[53]

The search and seizure crisis that arose in England and America was entirely and exclusively a *general warrant crisis*. There was no hint of concern on either side of the Atlantic with respect to warrantless searches. What Madison, Otis, and their American contemporaries wanted was to get rid of *statute-based* warrants, which Otis said violated "the fundamental principles of the [common] law." The affirmative goal was a return to the carefully restricted common law of search and seizure. (Searches in conjunction with arrests were common, and virtually nothing was made of them. It was originally assumed that this type of search had little to do with the Fourth Amendment.)

> [O]ur constitutional fathers were not concerned about warrantless searches, but about overreaching warrants. Far from looking at the warrant as a protection, they saw it as authority for unreasonable and oppressive searches, and sought to confine its issuance and execution in line with the stringent requirements applicable to common-law warrants for stolen goods. The language of the early constitutions amply bears out these conclusions. In all of them the warrant is treated as an enemy, not a friend.[54]

The goal of Madison and his associates was to control this enemy, not to extend it to areas that had never been troublesome. This is abundantly clear in the language of Madison's proposal and in the slightly altered version that the House adopted. The problem is that Madison's effort, thanks to Congressman Benson, became blurred.

---

53 *Entick v. Carrington*, State Trials, XIX, 1029 (1765); and *Wilkes v. Wood*, 98 Eng. Rep. 489 (1763).

54 Taylor, *Two Studies*, p. 41. See, for example, the Virginia Bill of Rights of 1776, Clause 10, and the Massachusetts Declaration of Rights of 1780, Article 14, quoted in Poore, *Federal and State Constitutions*.

> The right of the people to be secure in their persons, houses, papers, and effects, against
> unreasonable searches and seizures, shall not be violated, *and* (emphasis added) no
> Warrants shall issue, but upon probable cause, supported by Oath or affirmation, and
> particularly describing the place to be searched, and the persons or things to be seized.[55]

There in a single sentence are two disjointed, independent provisions: one promulgating a reasonableness test; the other a probable cause/warrant test. Whereas Madison's version makes clear the relationship between the two, Benson's leaves them dangling in ambiguity. That no doubt is why his terminology was decisively rejected in committee.

As originally drafted, the Fourth Amendment discussed only the essentials of a valid warrant. The wording "unreasonable searches and seizures" was not a clause of its own but rather a premise upon the first provision. Benson's alteration opened the door for a much broader interpretation of the Fourth Amendment. The general right to be secure against unreasonable searches and seizures was given its own clause, and thus the amendment outlaws more than the general warrant as originally drafted.

It is important, however, to realize that, while Benson's words are confusing, his purpose was clear. He did not seek to change the substance of Madison's proposal; he wanted only to emphasize its rejection of general warrants. His confusing alteration is not indicative of opposition to Madison's purpose, but rather to his style and phrasing. If we are to be guided by the intent of the framers, Benson included, there is no problem as to the basic meaning of the Fourth Amendment. It simply outlawed general warrants.

This brings us to the exclusion remedy for illegal searches and seizures. The Fourth Amendment and the self-incrimination clause of the Fifth Amendment have this in common: both put limits on police conduct with respect to the gathering of evidence. The one prohibits unreasonable searches and seizures, but provides no explicit sanction against violations thereof. The other, dealing with self-incrimination, has a built in exclusionary rule: no one "shall be compelled to

---

[55]   The Fourth Amendment of the United States Constitution.

be a *witness* against himself." In sum, compelled testimony is ruled out of court. The two amendments were adopted together as part of a single package, and they deal with the same problem, police misconduct. Why an exclusionary provision in the one, but not in the other?

Compulsion, for example, Star Chamber torture, may well produce false, i.e., unreliable, testimony. Thus the built-in exclusionary sanction (or remedy) in the Fifth Amendment followed an English tradition calculated to protect the accused from *unreliable evidence*.[56] But, unlike coerced testimony, the probative value of, for example, a pound of seized heroin or a murder weapon, is constant whether it was seized reasonably or unreasonably. Thus improperly obtained physical evidence, being no less reliable than that which is properly obtained (the Framers again following English tradition) did not rule it out.[57] Admission of reliable evidence, after all, endangers only guilty, not innocent people. Even the Warren Court, speaking through Justice Brennan, recognized and honored the *Adams-Bram* distinction between improperly obtained physical evidence and coerced, hence unreliable, spoken evidence.[58]

Omission of an explicit sanction in Amendment Four, and inclusion of one in Amendment Five, surely indicates the Framers thought they were dealing with two quite different problems. Certainly they did not contemplate that a sanction in the Fifth against unreliable evidence would carry back to Fourth Amendment reliable evidence cases. Madison, the father of both amendments, is famous as a highly rational man!

What then did the Framers contemplate as a sanction against unreasonable searches? Those who gave us the Fourth Amendment were the creatures of a proud, old common law tradition. One of its most basic tenets was that there can be no right without a remedy. "To assert that he has a right, and yet admit that he

---

[56]   *Bram v. United States,* 168 U.S. 532 (1897).

[57]   See *Adams v. New York*, 192 U.S. 585 (1904).

[58]   See *Schmerber v. California*, 384 U.S. 757 (1966) and *United States v. Wade*, 383 U.S. 218 (1967).

has no remedy, appears rather paradoxical."[59] This seemed so obvious that Chief Justice John Marshall could accept as "a settled and invariable principle [of Anglo-American law] that every right, when withheld must have a remedy, and every injury its redress."[60] For those steeped in the common law tradition, as were our early ancestors,[61] the declaration of a limited right of privacy in the Fourth Amendment necessarily entailed a corresponding remedy or sanction for its enforcement. But what enforcing mechanism did our ancestors contemplate? Since they did not explicitly provide one, such as in the Fifth Amendment, it would seem inevitable that they had in mind a common law remedy.[62] Note Justice Story's observation less than fifty years after the writing of the Fourth Amendment, that "it [the Fourth Amendment] is little more than the affirmance of a great constitutional doctrine of the common law."[63] Since there can be no search and seizure of physical goods without a trespass, the ancient and well-known common law action for trespass comes readily to mind. In fact the *Wilkes* and *Entick* cases were trespass actions for damages against the king's searching agents. This litigation and the ancient trespass tradition on which it was based were well known in colonial America. The Framers, it would seem, simply did what came naturally with respect to the Fourth Amendment, so naturally as to need no expression or elaboration. They took for granted the major postulates of their legal inheritance, just as we do with respect to ours. If on the other hand, an exclusion sanction to control police misconduct in the Fourth Amendment had been contemplated, it would have required explicit formulation just as in the Fifth

---

[59]   Justice Johnson in *Fairfax Devisee v. Hunter's Lessee*, 7 Cranch 603 (1813). Also see Sir William Blackstone's *Commentaries*, 4 vols. (Philadelphia: R. Welsch and Co., 1902), 3, 1765, n.23.

[60]   *Marbury v. Madison,* 1 Cranch 137 (1803).

[61]   See Roscoe Pound, *Criminal Justice in America* (New York: H. Holt, 1930), p. 82.

[62]   See Bradford Wilson, "Enforcing the Fourth Amendment: The Original Understanding," 28 Catholic Lawyer 173 (1983); Alfred Hill, "Constitutional Remedies," 69 *Columbia Law Review* 1109 (1969).

[63]   Blackstone, *Commentaries*, p. 748.

Amendment. A Fourth Amendment exclusionary rule could not have been taken for granted, for the gambit was unknown in Anglo-American law until much later.[64] The stark, irreducible fact is that for more than one hundred years we relied upon common law remedies for vindication of Fourth Amendment rights.[65] The adequacy of that approach was not even questioned by the Supreme Court until 1886 in *Boyd v. United States*.[66]

Boyd is famous because, if only by dicta it suggested that "the Fourth and Fifth Amendments run almost into each other." The thought was that personal papers obtained even in a reasonable search should be excluded by virtue of their capacity to incriminate in violation of the Fifth Amendment. There are several difficulties in this. As we have seen, the foundation of the Fifth Amendment exclusionary rule is that coerced confessions are inherently unreliable because of the coercion and pressure used to obtain them. But the reliability of physical papers is not diminished by seizure however gross. Wigmore in his famous treatise on evidence doubted the alliance of the two amendments.[67] The underlying distinction between the two turns upon the reliability of the evidence. Moreover, the Fourth Amendment outlaws only unreasonable searches while permitting those that are reasonable. Yet the Fifth Amendment exclusion remedy is all encompassing and absolute. To transpose the Fifth Amendment exclusion provision to search and seizure is to preclude even reasonable searches. *Boyd* has

---

[64]   Apart from the intimations in *Boyd v. United States*, 116 U.S. 616 (1886) the exclusionary rule seems to have originated in *State v. Sheridan*, 121 Iowa 164, 96 N. W. 730 (1903).

[65]   It is basic in the common law system that any common law rule may be altered, revoked, or replaced by legislation.

[66]   116 U.S. 616 (1886).

[67]   John H. Wigmore, *A Treatise on the Anglo-American System of Evidence in Trial's at Common Law*, 5 vols., 2nd ed. (Boston: Little, Brown, and Co., 1923), Sections 2184, 2250, 2263-64.

not survived,[68] but it is crucial because it eased the way for transposing the bad evidence rule to good evidence cases.[69]

The transposition itself came in *Weeks v. United States*[70] about a century and a quarter after adoption of the Fourth Amendment.[71] Weeks was suspected of sending lottery tickets in the mail. Two searches took place, one by local officials and the other by federal agents. Weeks petitioned the Court for the return of his property prior to trial on the ground that it had been seized illegally. The Supreme Court declared the seizure by the federal officers illegal and ordered the return of the seized evidence. The seizure by state officials was not disturbed: the Fourth Amendment and the exclusionary rule then applied only in federal cases.

Why the Court selected exclusion as the favored remedy over others is unclear. Many theories were available. *Weeks* set the stage for the modern development of the Fourth Amendment by triggering reform in the treatment of evidence. Some states adopted the new federal rule, or a limited version of it; others used different remedies.[72] Police departments also made changes in their procedures for obtaining evidence. Most importantly, *Weeks* was the catalyst that made search warrants a common tool of law enforcement.

---

[68]   See, for example, *Fisher v. United States*, 425 U.S. 391 (1976); *United States v. Wade*, 388 U.S. 218 (1967), *Schmerber v. California*, 384 U.S. 757 (1966).

[69]   Ironically, the *Boyd* reasoning reemerged if only for a moment in a most unusual context. Justice Black, the fifth and deciding vote in *Mapp*, argued on Fourth and Fifth Amendment grounds that the Court should impose the exclusionary rule in all state cases.

[70]   232 U.S. 383 (1914).

[71]   The Supreme Court in the early twentieth century could hardly be considered a bastion of civil liberty. In fact it was a stronghold for property and laissez-faire interests. Virtually all national, criminal legislation at the time would by its nature apply mainly to business operations. In that context the exclusion principle would be a special boon for laissez-faire business interests, as, for example, in both the Boyd and Weeks cases. Note this comment (reaction) by the Roosevelt Court in *Beard v. Alexandria*, 341 U.S. 622 (1951): "The exigencies of trade are not ordinarily expected to have a higher rating constitutionally than the tranquility of the fireside."

[72]   E. Gangi, "The Exclusionary Rule: A Case Study in Judicial Usurpation," 34 *Drake Law Review* 33 (1984), 46-47.

Enthusiasm for the *Weeks* rule has had its limits. Counsel's efforts to get a *Weeks* exclusion in state cases were repudiated time after time, perhaps most vividly by the Roosevelt Court in *Wolf v. Colorado*.[73] There the justices were unanimous in holding that

> The security of one's privacy against arbitrary intrusion by the police—which is the core of the Fourth Amendment—is basic to a free society. It is therefore "implicit in the concept of ordered liberty" and as such enforceable against the States through the Due Process Clause [of the Fourteenth Amendment.]

But, for the *Wolf* Court, *exclusion* of reliable, objective evidence was quite another matter. While the privacy right was deemed "basic to a free society," the *Weeks* remedy was not. The majority found this distinction not simply in its own value system, but in the practice of a great majority of the world's fifty-eight English language jurisdictions.[74] Thus for the Roosevelt Court and most of the Anglo-American world, as seemingly for James Madison et al. the proper remedy was to be found in the common law (supplemented by such legislation as the community might think appropriate).

However, on the eve of Dollree Mapp's trial for possessing obscene material, the consideration of remedies for the Fourth Amendment were being revived. Certain that *Wolf* was merely a stepping stone, some of the justices, particularly Tom Clark, were ready to take the leap to a specific remedy for Fourth violations. In just a decade since *Wolf*, exclusion became the norm for search and seizure violations by state police officers. Since 1914, the same had been true of violations by federal searching agents.

In Cleveland, this mattered little for Mapp and Delau. Mapp would soon stand trial for violating the state's tough obscenity statute. Out on bail, she prepared for

---

[73]   38 U.S. 25 (1949).

[74]   Frankfurter noted in his majority opinion in *Wolf* that only sixteen states had adopted the remedy of exclusion to address search and seizure violations. 338 U.S. 25 (1949). 753 U. S. 643 (1961).

trial and continued her daily routine. Delau and Haney continued to investigate policy and with the help of Donald King, would later charge Shondor Birns and his associates for the bombing. The law of search and seizure, crucial and relevant to those who would consider the matter on Milverton Road, was irrelevant to those locally. Cleveland was focused on the policy and gaming underworld. The trial of Birns and the star witness King were front page news. It appeared that no one in Cleveland, except perhaps the local chapter of the American Civil Liberties Union, was connecting the legal developments of search and seizure law to the city's local events.

CHAPTER FIVE
The Trial

The dusty old file is stamped, dated, marked on, and a bit mutilated. It lacks the glitter of history or of constitutional struggle. It was not preserved as a part of the legacy of rights that originated in such a simple lawsuit: "Case number 36091 the STATE OF OHIO, versus Dollree Mapp."Although the state's notation was preprinted and a clerk typist added the defendant's name, the case seems intimidating by nature of the state appearing so prominently in the title. Dollree Mapp's arrest card, on file with the Cleveland Police Department, notes the following:

Mapp Dollree (name)	68326 (number)
4786 Lee Rd (address)	6/28/57 (date)

Sex   Age 28   Race N

Charge   Poss. Of Obscene Pictures and Books

Transcript   Cleveland

Consolidation

So defendant No. 68326, so noted on this dilapidated case file, is prosecuted in the Cuyahoga County Court of Common Pleas. The file cover reveals the long history of *Mapp v. Ohio*. In barely legible script, and with abbreviations, it is noted:

7-8-58 Ch pleas to G.
8-1-58 Deft withdraws plea of guilty.
Pleas not guilty. Same
9-4-58 Verdict G
P.F.S . Lybarger J.
9-10-58 Sentenced to OS Ref for Women
                                            Lybarger, J.

An imposing stamp states: F I L E D
                                    Court of Appeals
                                    Oct 8 1958

and at the top of the file noted in hand is:

C of A 24699

Stamped askew is: F I L E D
            Apr 2 1959
        SUPREME COURT OF OHIO [1]

---

[1]   Original document, Cleveland Court of Common Pleas, Microfilm. This entire section is taken from this original trial transcript. Old case files are kept in a warehouse in Cleveland. The Mapp case file was buried beneath scores of other cases, misfiled. I was fortunate and persistent enough to find it. This entire chapter is taken from this document.

These notes and abbreviations give a shorthand version of the acrimonious struggle that would not reach the Supreme Court of the United States for three years. A twenty-eight-year-old black, or in those days, Negro, woman is charged with violating the state of Ohio's obscenity statute. She initially pleads guilty, then changes her plea to not guilty. In a brief trial she is found guilty and is sentenced to a seven-year term in the Ohio State Reformatory for Women by Judge Lybarger. Within a month of her conviction, Dollree Mapp appeals her case to the Ohio State Court of Appeals. By 1959 she is before the Ohio Supreme Court, and in the fall of 1960 she continues forward, now with the help of the Cleveland office of the American Civil Liberties Union.

~~~

The state of Ohio, through Cuyahoga County and the City of Cleveland, set forth to prosecute Dollree Mapp in the fall of 1957. Affidavits were filed before the deputy clerk of the Cleveland Municipal Court, authenticating deposed statements of Officer Haney and Officer Delau that indeed "Dollree Mapp did unlawfully have in her possession and under her control certain lewd, obscene, and lascivious books and pictures." These statements were dated May 25, 1957. The sheriff, Joseph M. Sweeney, submitted fees for reimbursement with regard to subpoenas served in the Mapp case on August 27, 1958. The sheriff wanted to be repaid for the cost of issuing subpoenas to Patrolman Michael Haney and Sergeant Carl Delau and Sergeant Michael Dever and P.W. Betty Anthony (Police Woman) of the Women's Bureau. Noting on the form, "Service and Return: Ben McDonald," the deputy sheriff wrote 100, and next to "Miles Travel" 32, for a total of 132.

By September of 1958 the case was headed for trial. Foreshadowing what was to come, in the Court of Common Pleas Case Number 68326 State of Ohio Plaintiff vs. Dolly Mapp, Mapp's attorney filed a motion to suppress. A. L. Kearns requested the court to suppress the evidence obtained "to wit: certain claimed lewd and lascivious books, pictures, and photographs and intended to be used in evidence in the trial of the aforesaid cause." His reason was "that the aforesaid evidence was not procured by a proper search warrant as provided by Section 2905.35 of the Ohio Revised Code." The word "provided" had been written in over the typed word "submitted." The motion was filed with the court on September 3, 1958.

The court set the hearing for Kearns's motion for Court Room No.1 of the Court of Common Pleas Criminal Division. Readily, Mapp's motion was overruled. Also on September 3rd the court amended the indictment to note Mapp's correct name as "Dollree" rather than "Dolly." Before Judge Donald F. Lybarger were the prosecuting attorney, John T. Corrigan, and Gertrude Mahon the assistant prosecutor; Dollree Mapp who was brought into court in the custody of the sheriff, Al Kearns; the court reporter; and the empaneled jury. The jury was composed of six women and six men. Those twelve individuals were Louise E. Barthold, Theresa G. Arra, Elizabeth Ann Atkinson, Jas. Richard Barton, Thos. J. Ganagan, Margaret Bandel, Fred Hashagen, John F. Kovacs, Chas. A. Kensig, Virginia M. Bender, Richard J. Kendall, and Ruth Brezina. They were to assemble in Courtroom Number 1 of the Court of Common Pleas, Criminal Branch, beginning September 3, 1958.

~~~

The first issue for Judge Lybarger to contend with, ironically, was the search of the Mapp residence. Although the focal point of the charges was the obscenity statute and the possession of obscene material, Al Kearns, like every good lawyer, was arguing all lines of defense that would possibly free his client. He began by expressing his view that the Ohio Code Section 2905.35 interpreted by the Ohio Supreme Court in *Lindway v. Ohio* required a search warrant to obtain the evidence seized from his client, Dollree Mapp. The prosecutor, Gertrude Mahon, responded that she had not read *Lindway* recently but that it did not require a search warrant be obtained in order to seize evidence. Judge Lybarger got to the heart of the issue, at least the eventual turning point of the case, rather quickly.

> The court: Was a warrant issued in this case?
> Mrs. Mahon: Yes, your honor, a search warrant was issued. ...They did have
> a search warrant and obtained this evidence as a result of it.

Kearns does not dispute this but claims that warrants were not blanket search warrants and surely did not specify "the lascivious pictures they expect to use in evidence." Judge Lybarger then gave his interpretation of *Lindway*. He stated that *Lindway* in parts four and five noted that a motion to suppress and the possible exclusion of evidence is separate from the method used to procure the evidence. In other words, if the admissibility of evidence has been settled (through the obtainment of a search warrant) then the court need not entertain the collateral issue of how the evidence was obtained. The *Lindway* court was concerned with the admissibility of the evidence, not the method used to obtain it. Of course, the Supreme Court would view these issues as logically connected. Merely obtaining a warrant was not enough. How the search was conducted was important as well. This subtle distinction was the difference between a legal and illegal search, as the Supreme Court of the United States would view it. However, for Judge Lybarger, in agreeing with Ohio law and the Ohio Supreme Court interpretation, obtaining a proper search warrant truncated the inquiry by the court. Whether the search warrant stipulated one item but another was found, or whether the police were aggressive or not, were of no consequence in the Fourth Amendment question. Hence, the first inquiry by a court of law into the actions of Delau and company would be as it always was. Settled in law and practice, Kearns's request, taking up little more than three pages of the trial transcript, was denied. The jury, now empaneled and sworn in, began with opening statements of both Mrs. Mahon and Mr. Kearns.

The State of Ohio began by putting Officer Michael Haney on the witness stand. Gertie Mahon led him through the particulars of his name, address, and job description. Her intention was to introduce into evidence all the obscene materials found at the Mapp home. He stated for the record that he recalled going to the house on Milverton Road that day in May of 1957. He stated that he arrived at the house about 1:30 P.M. He was asked if he had encountered the defendant, Dollree Mapp. Affirming that he had, Haney pointed toward Mapp who was seated beside A. L. Kearns. Haney was well acquainted with the defendant, noting that he was familiar with her as Dollree Mapp or Dollree Bivens. Officer Haney recounted that the reason for their visit to Mapp's home was that

> on that particular day we had received information from a confidential source that there was a person hiding out in the home, who was wanted for questioning in connection with a recent bombing, and that there was a large amount of policy paraphernalia being hidden in the home, either in the basement or the suite on the second floor.

Haney also explained that when the officers rang the bell to the second floor apartment on the side of the dwelling, Mapp peered from the window and responded to their request of entry by saying "I'll call my attorney, Mr. Green, and see if he thinks I should let you in." She left her window perch briefly and then returned to tell them that "I have been advised by my attorney not to let you in without a search warrant." As the record reflects, according to Haney, "A search warrant was brought out after an hour and a half or two hour delay, brought to the premises, and the officers were admitted by Mrs. Mapp from the sidewalk."

Haney then explained in detail the nature of the search of Mapp's home. While thorough, it did not seem abusive. He noted that they entered each room and searched it. He searched a dresser located near one of the beds in the upstairs bedroom. In it he found four books. He stated that when he removed them, Mrs. Mapp who was sitting on the bed watching as the search progressed said, " Better not look at those; they might excite you." Haney then looked at the items and deemed them to be obscene. In a suitcase in the room he found "photo albums and a pencil drawing on paper of a very obscene nature." Sergeant Delau also found a "separate group of vulgar pictures." Altogether according to Haney, the police were in the Mapp home for "two and a half or three hours." All the items were entered into evidence, State's Exhibits 1, 2, 3, and 4. State's Exhibit 1 was the book, *The Affairs of the Troubador*. Exhibit 2 was the book *Little Darlings*. State Exhibit 3 was *London Stage Affairs* and Exhibit 4 was *Memories of a Hotel Man*. The obscene pencil drawing was entered in as Exhibit 5. The photos and personal papers from the suitcase were Exhibit 6. Exhibit 7 consisted of more drawings, a diet slip, and pictures of Dollree Mapp. Exhibits 8 and 9 were photographs of Dolly and several others at the Chatterbox Musical Bar and Grill. Exhibits 10, 11, 12, and 13 were obscene pictures found in various locations in the home.

With that, Officer Haney's direct testimony ended. The prosecutor had not asked for any details about how the warrant was procured or made any mention of how the items seized from Mapp's home were obtained, only that they were. With little fanfare, the damning evidence, obscene material, had been entered into evidence. The focal point of the prosecution was the nature of the items seized, not the methods used to seize them. For Gertrude Mahon, the trial was about violating Ohio's obscenity statute, and for her it appeared an open and shut case.

As expected, A. L. Kearns focused on the search itself. He very quickly asked Officer Haney particulars about the search warrant.

> Kearns: And did you procure a search warrant?
> Haney: I did not, no.
> Kearns: Well, some of the officers?
> Haney: That's right.
> Kearns: But when the search was made there were more officers than you
> and Sergeant Delau and Patrolman Dever that were there?
> Haney: That's right.
> Kearns: How many all together?
> Haney: There was Sergeant Delau, Patrolman Dever, Lieutenant White come
> with a search warrant; Inspector Carl Bare of the Fourth District was there;
> the Captain was there; it could be the Captain was there; I am not certain.
> Kearns: Who else?

Haney: There was a patrolman from one of the zone cars there.
Kearns: That is seven?
Haney: Yes.

Kearns went into some detail about the actual moment that items were found and by whom and where. At one point, he insinuated that material could have been planted because Haney did not actually see the obscene items coming out of the chest of drawers being searched by Sergeant Delau because Delau was facing away. Kearns also tried to imply that the suitcase that contained many items found by Haney was actually being used by Morris Jones. Kearns attempted to get Haney to admit that a standard text book of cosmetology had the name "Morris Jones" inscribed on it. He also argued that a gun was found in the suitcase that was owned by Morris Jones. But Haney held firm to his story. He had not seen items from anyone else in the suitcase or room.

Kearns then vainly focused on the search of Mapp's basement, which had produced a trunk of policy paraphernalia. Kearns tried to get Haney to admit that at one point all seven police officers were in the home of Mapp, culling for evidence. Haney, experienced and clearly wise to the tack that Kearns was taking, argued that he was only knowledgeable about his search area he covered with Sergeant Delau, the bedroom, and that he had no knowledge of what went on in the basement. On redirect and recross, the first mention of any physical restraint to Mapp was made.

Kearns: Officer, isn't it a fact that Mrs. Mapp was handcuffed to one of the uniformed police officers while the search was going on?
Haney: Mrs. Mapp was handcuffed, but there was a uniformed officer there; I couldn't testify whether she was handcuffed to him or merely handcuffed.

Immediately, Mrs. Mahon countered the faintest suggestion that Dollree Mapp was physically mistreated.

Mahon: Do you know, officer, the reason why she was handcuffed?
Kearns: Object.
The court: He may answer, the reason.
Haney: She was handcuffed because she tore the search warrant out of the officer's hands and placed it down into her bosom, and he tried to get it back, got into a tussle trying to get it back.
Mahon: She got into a tussle with the police officers?
Haney: Yes.

In retrospect, the most important interchange for the history-making case of *Mapp v. Ohio* was about to take place. Dollree Mapp's attorney, A. L. Kearns, asked Officer Haney, simply and point blank:

Kearns: Where is that search warrant?
Haney: I don't know.
Kearns: Do you have it here?
Haney: I don't have it.
Kearns: Would you tell the jury who has it?
Haney: I won't tell the jury who has it; no sir.

Upon her chance to question, Mahon quickly tried to shift the blame.

Mahon: You yourself did not obtain the search warrant, did you, officer?
Haney: No, I did not.
Kearns: Do you know who did?
Haney: I was told Lieutenant White obtained it.

With that, Officer Michael Haney was dismissed and the exhibits were entered into evidence.

This would prove to be *the most* critical point for future litigation. The fact that the state could never produce the warrant was damaging. Even producing a flawed warrant or the affidavit that supported it would have tipped the scales of justice in favor of Mapp. The constable would be proven to have blundered, hence the windfall to the criminal. So rather than the legal struggle moving into the intricacies of the warrant and its contents, the issues were clear. While the state could not produce a warrant, it argued it had obtained one. The defense, while it could not point to a flawed warrant or even a bogus piece of paper, was left attacking the unseen in hopes of creating reasonable doubt.

Gertrude Mahon quickly followed Officer Haney with Sergeant Carl Delau. He also began his testimony giving his name, address, rank, and a brief work history with the Cleveland Police Department. Delau quickly got to the details of the search of Map's home and the struggle over the search warrant. He recounted:

> When we told her we had a search warrant she opened the door. Before that she said she wouldn't; at that time we did pry the screen door to gain entrance to the building itself. We went upstairs, myself and Lieutenant White; Inspector Bare had arrived on the scene. She demanded to see the warrant; that is when she grabbed it out of his hand and concealed it on her person. We recovered the warrant, and she was quite belligerent at that particular time.

Delau also added that Dollree Map was present during the complete search of the bedroom. He included that the entire second floor of the home was searched and that only items pertaining to the personal effects of a female adult and a female child were found. In other words, the contention by Dollree that the obscene material found belonged to her most recent border, Morris Jones, was unsubstantiated by the items found in the home. "After we brought her down to Central Station we questioned her again, and it was there she said those books were left behind by Morris Jones, who had lived with her before that and who had roomed at her home on Milverton Road." Delau also noted that the basement was searched. A large footlocker containing policy paraphernalia was found. "There was an awful lot of policy paraphernalia, five books of policy polls, policy slips, result slips, for the California and interstate policy houses, and other things that belonged to that, and slip staple racks, regular crayons, slips on which pictures had been crayoned."

Mahon: Was there any name on that box of crayons?
Delau: Yes.
Mahon: What was the name?
Delau: The name on the box was Barbara Bivens.

On cross, Sergeant Delau was quickly questioned about his prior knowledge of Mapp, Kearns trying to paint the picture that Delau had it in for Dollree, and the continued pursuit of her smacked of police harassment. On the specifics of the warrant, Delau was asked precisely how a warrant was obtained.

Kearns: And then she told you that you better get a search warrant, then you could go into her house?
Delau: Correct.
Kearns: And it was then that you called Lieutenant White and told him you were having trouble getting in, and she insists on a search warrant?
Delau: I didn't call White; I called Lieutenant Cooney, my boss.
Kearns: Then sometime later when you and the other two police officers were on the scene, someone came out with a search warrant, didn't they?
Delau: That is correct.
Kearns: And who was it?
Delau: That was Lieutenant White.
Kearns: Lieutenant White came with a search warrant?
Delau: Yes.

Again the jury and court were quickly exposed to the most central fact for the Supreme Court of the United States; not if the material seized from Dollree Mapp was obscene, but the nature of the seizure itself. In the course of laying the groundwork for the material entered into evidence, both Mahon and Kearns revealed and exposed the Fourth Amendment problem that was to become the future focal point of this case.

Both Haney and Delau testified that a search warrant was obtained. Both testified that it was obtained by Lieutenant Tommy White. Both testified that the search and seizure of Mapp's house did not begin before the warrant was brought to the premises and presented to the defendant. Thus the search of Dollree Mapp was the *result* of police procedure to procure a search warrant. As would later be revealed, both the spirit of the request for a search warrant and the process to obtain it, met the standard of due process in 1957. Some would argue, it exceeded it. The suspect requested a warrant, the police obtained one, and did not commence searching until the warrant was presented to the defendant. It is only in retrospect that the search of Mapp becomes flawed and seen as unlawful. The actions of the police on May 23rd appear to be standard and no more aggressive or invasive than the commonly accepted practice. The search of Milverton Road was unusual in that the police did obtain a search warrant rather than search without one. It was unusual for the procedural care taken rather than the lack of it. The facts of the search simply do not reveal the police misconduct that is associated with Fourth Amendment violations. As revealed much later, to Officers Delau, Haney, White, Cooney, and the district attorney, John T. Corrigan, there was a Fourth Amendment violation, but one of a more technical than physical nature.

A few moments later, with a brief redirect by Mrs. Mahon and a few more questions by Mr. Kearns, the State of Ohio rested its case against Dollree Mapp. Two witnesses, both police officers, testified to the motive of searching Mapp's house, the procedure they took to do so, the search itself, and the results of their efforts. The testimony was straightforward. In little over fifty pages of trial transcript, the state had made its case against Dollree Mapp for possession of obscene material. It would take her about the same amount of time and transcript space to attempt to defend herself.

Mr. Kearns's first witness was his legal partner Walter Green. Green painted a rather different picture from the state's depiction of a routine search. Green stated that he spoke to Mapp several times on May 23, 1957. She had called him saying her house was surrounded by police who wanted to gain admission and should she let them in. I said, "If they can produce a warrant, and show you that warrant, let you read it to see it is in proper order, then let them in." Eventually after several telephone calls from Mapp, Green decided to go to her home. "As I drove up I saw several police cars and what appeared to me policemen all over the place."

> Kearns asked his law partner: "At this time can you give this jury some idea of how many policemen you saw, as you say, all over the place?"
> Green: My estimate at this time would be ten to fifteen officers.

Green noted that as best he recalled, "half to two-thirds of the men present were in uniform." He continued on, "Well, it was difficult finding a parking place right in front of the house, and I pulled up possibly a house or two beyond hers. As I walked back a couple of officers started to walk toward me, then they turned around and walked back, and I saw Sergeant Delau, I believe, attempting to kick in the door." Green identified Carl Delau and stated that he informed the officer that there was no need to use force to enter. If he had a warrant, merely show it to Mrs. Mapp. "He said he had a warrant; they refused to show it to anybody. I never did see a warrant." Kearns, through Green, was attempting to leave the impression that a warrant never existed.

Here the versions of the search radically diverge. Green testified that a much more serious violation took place than portrayed by the state. After Sergeant Delau tried to kick in the door, "He got a sharp instrument—I mean a metallic instrument; I don't know what it was—and broke the glass in the door and somebody reached in and opened the door and let them in." Green continued his description of excessive force. He stated that as the officers poured into the Mapp residence, he was forced to stay behind. Upon instructions from Inspector Bare, a uniformed captain was instructed to keep Green from entering the home. "As I recall now the captain opened his tunic, and I got a glimpse of a revolver that he had on his belt." Repeated requests for entry were met with repeated denials. The tone of the encounter is vastly different than that in Haney's and Delau's version. Whereas the officers argued the entry was routine, here Green indicated that the police threatened him, at least implied, and used physical force to enter the Mapp home. The search, according to Green, was aggressive, threatening, and a clear abuse of police power.

Green continued. He stated that from his location outside the house, he could hear commotion and loud talk. "I heard Mrs. Mapp call out several times." One time she said "Take your hand out of my dress."

Green saw or heard little else until the search was completed. He witnessed the officers taking Dollree Mapp to the police car. He could not recall if she was handcuffed but noted that she was placed in the backseat. Seated next to her for the ride to Central Police Station was Sergeant Carl Delau. Green had little else to add, and Kearns completed his direct examination of his law partner.

The cross examination of Walter Green was uneventful, primarily because given his limited vantage point, he could provide no particulars of the search of the Mapp home. He stated that he was present to observe the events since Mapp was "terrified and asked that I come out." He had heard the statement of the police reaching into her dress, but could not state what events caused her to say that. Green did reveal that he had come to the Mapp house with a camera and took some pictures. Unfortunately, no film survived to document the events of May 23, 1957.[2] Green admitted that he mishandled his camera and that the exposed film was of trees rather than the scene of the search. Green did provide one piece of important information. He stated that he observed two individuals standing by the police, Dollree Mapp and Virgil Ogletree. "I saw him [Ogletree] the first time in the downstairs suite."[3] So the tip had paid off for the

---

[2] When I heard that photographs were taken of the Mapp search, I could not believe my fortune! I contacted the offices of Walter Green and A. L. Kearns and was told that the photographs were gone, perhaps missing or destroyed. I pursued them for many months through the police department evidence lab and through the law offices and families. It was only through the cross-examination of Walter Green I learned that the camera was not used correctly and the only photographs taken were of "trees and scenes, and the double exposure of the sergeant" (p. 60 of the original trial transcript). To my knowledge, these were discarded as irrelevant, since they failed to document the events.

[3] Original trial transcript of *Mapp v. Ohio*, Court of Common Pleas, Criminal Division, p. 63.

police. They had found someone with information on the King bombing at the Mapp home. In addition, they had found evidence of policymaking and carted off a large chest and other policy paraphernalia along with Dollree Mapp and Virgil Ogletree to the Central Police Station.

Kearns's next witness was Dolores Clark, an acquaintance of Dollree's whose testimony focused on the obscene materials. She indicated that she had come over to help Mapp clean up a room and in the course of doing so, they found "a bunch of dirty books and some pictures." Clark said that Dollree commented upon finding them, "Look at what filthy stuff men read." The materials were bagged and taken to the basement. Clark indicated that the items were not Mapp's and were being stored by her. On-cross examination, Gertrude Mahon called into question the witness's inability to remember specifics, particularly the month or date of the events. Yet Clark offered some support of Mapp's version of the evidence seized.

Kearns then chose to put Dollree Mapp on the witness stand. Whether she insisted upon testifying or her lawyer felt it necessary in order to win is not clear. The bulk of the testimony in support of her would come from Dollree herself. The direct and cross-examinations were long and thorough. What is revealed is a woman who is steadfast in her story. She never wavered in making her argument. The obscene materials were not hers but belonged to her former tenant, Morris Jones. The items were not found in the chest of drawers in her bedroom but in a box in the basement that she had prepared for Mr. Jones to retrieve at some later date. Dollree Mapp carefully and artfully laid out the events of that day for the jury. She was straightforward. Gertie Mahon could not rattle her. The words of her testimony leap off the transcript pages. Dollree Mapp, bright and well spoken, asserted her innocence with some authority. She showed no doubt, no remorse, no sense of guilt. Just as the officers who searched her were believable, so was Dollree Mapp.

"Give us your full name, please."
"Dollree Mapp"

"Spell the first name."

"D-o-l-l-r-e-e."

Dollree recounted the initial facts of the events of May 23rd much as the others had. About 1:30 P.M. someone rang her doorbell. It was the three police officers: Delau, Haney, and Dever. She asked them what they wanted, and they said they wanted to question her. She called her attorney and was advised to not let them in without a warrant. She was asked by her attorney if there was any additional information concerning the warrant. She answered: "No. He (Green) told me to make sure that it was a search warrant, and they should let me see it and read it, and then I should let them in." She informed Delau of this and he told her he would have his boss, Lieutenant Cooney, call her. He did, and she told him the same thing and then hung up on him.

When the police came to the door, indicating they had a warrant, she said, "Inspector, I want to see the search warrant." He said, "Here is the search warrant." She testified that "he held it back from me, and I remember Mr. Green told me I should see it and read it, and I told him I wanted to see it. He said, 'You can't see it.' At that I reached over, took the search warrant from his hand, and put it down in my bosom."

The testimony got more and more colorful. Dollree testified that there were at least a dozen police officer along with a "paddy wagon." With the warrant down her dress, one officer asked, "What are we going to do now?" Dollree replied, "The one that grabbed me said, 'I'm going down after it.' I said, 'No, you are not.' He went down anyway."

When asked why she took such drastic action with the warrant, she replied, "Because Mr. Green told me I should read it, and I wanted to read it to make sure it was a search warrant."

Then Dollree testified that she was grabbed, her arms were twisted, and some lieutenant behind her asked for handcuffs and handcuffed her to him and later to a uniformed officer. Other police were going upstairs as well as downstairs to search. As the search continued, Mapp was taken upstairs where, with handcuffs, she sat on the bed. There, she watched Officer Delau search her chest of drawers. About that time Officer Haney walked in with a brown paper bag and asked whether the items inside belonged to Dollree. She testified that he better not look because the items might embarrass him, in contradistinction to assertions of the sexual innuendo arousing or "exciting" him. She denied to Officer Haney that they belonged to her. He responded: "Oh yes, that's the kind of trash you read."

The crux of the Mapp defense was taking shape. Dollree Mapp testified that all the items that the state had entered into evidence were found in her home, but that they belonged to a boarder, Morris Jones. Jones had gone to New York on vacation and had decided not to return. In the course of cleaning up and packing away his belongings she came across the items that were obscene. Mapp testified that she had packed them up and placed them in the basement, contradicting the word of the police who testified that the items were found in Mapp's room among her personal belongings.

> Kearns: Do these State Exhibits 1, 2, 3, and 4, and Exhibits 10, 11, 12, and
> 13, belong to you?
> Mapp: No.
> Kearns: Did you ever own them?
> Mapp: No.
> Kearns: Did you ever have possession of them?
> Mapp: No.

She testified that the items she placed in her suitcase belonged to Morris Jones such as the obscene drawings and the handgun. Indeed all the items in question were owned by Jones, and Mapp had only briefly encountered them when storing his belongings.

Later she was asked, "Were you ever given an opportunity to read that search warrant?" "I never had—I never read one word on there," she replied. After disavowing owning or possessing any of the evidence that the State had entered into evidence as exhibits one through thirteen, Mr. Kearns ended his direct examination.

Gertrude Mahon tried to shake Mapp off her version of the location in which all the obscene items were found. She did not succeed. Mapp remained firm to her version of events, more or less calling the police liars.

> Mahon: Now you heard Officer Delau testify that he found these four groups
> of pictures in a dresser drawer in your bedroom?
> Mapp: Yes.
> Mahon: You heard him testify to that?
> Mapp: Yes.
> Mahon: Is he telling the truth?
> Kearns: Object, if the court please.
> The court: She may answer that.
> Mapp: So far as I am concerned he is not.

Mapp continued to tussle with Mahon about the items seized, their alleged owner Morris Jones, and Jones's whereabouts. Dollree Mapp stuck to her story. She never wavered. Her objection was to indicate to the jury that the items were not her property and that she was merely storing them for a renter to retrieve at a later date.

Of course her credibility would have been bolstered by the presence of Morris Jones. Coming forward to claim material that was under prosecution because of its obscene nature was unlikely. Mapp's contention that the items did not belong to her but to someone else was unsupported with additional testimony or evidence linking Jones to the items. It was her word against that of the police. The state presented evidence of a routine search where the police even went the extra mile to obtain a search warrant. Mapp's version of events characterized the search as overly aggressive and abusive.

The jury was given these two different stories in just one day of testimony, September 3rd. In the annals of American criminal law, the case was by all standards uneventful. The police had information about a suspect and they followed the lead up with a search. This was not unusual in 1957. So the six men and women of Cleveland who heard the case of the state of Ohio versus Dollree Mapp, if asked, would never have believed that this case would be appealed to the Supreme Court of the United States. They would never have believed that the case of *Mapp v. Ohio* would become a landmark case, taught in every criminal law course in the United States even today. They would never believe that the application of the exclusionary rule to every jurisdiction in the United States would be the result of the case against Dollree Mapp. It was a local dispute involving the vices of gambling and pornography.

On Thursday, September 4, 1958, at 9:15 A.M.., the trial resumed with closing arguments. When both Mahon and Kearns were finished, Judge Lybarger charged the jury with its criteria to apply to the facts at hand. His instructions were typical. The definition of evidence, the way in which juries should evaluate testimony from the witness stand, statement from counsel, and rulings from the bench. Judge Lybarger read the indictment against Mapp. She has "knowingly had in her possession and under her control certain lewd and lascivious books, pictures, and photographs, said books, pictures and photographs being so indecent and immoral in their nature that the same would be offensive to the court and improper to be placed upon the records thereof." Lybarger informed the jury that the plea entered by the defendant was "not guilty." Lybarger reminded them that "the plea of not guilty entered by the defendant clothes her with the legal presumption of innocence. This presumption is not a mere matter of form, but is rather a shield which the law throws about the defendant." He continued: "The presumption of innocence is only overcome when you, the jury, find the evidence is such as to exclude every reasonable doubt of the guilt of the defendant." The law required the judge to read the jury the statutory definition of reasonable doubt.

> It is not a mere possible doubt because everything relating to human affairs or depending upon moral evidence is open to some possible or imaginary doubt. It is that state of the case which, after an entire comparison and consideration of all the evidence, leaves the minds of the jurors in that condition that they cannot say they feel an abiding conviction to a moral certainty of the truth of the charge.

The judge then read the specific portions of the Ohio statute that pertained to obscenity. The key phrases were that the person knowingly possessed or had under their control obscene items. Specifically the state had to prove that the act was done knowingly rather than accidentally. The judge explained that the items had to be in her possession or under her control, meaning "the act of holding or keeping it." "Neither possession or control necessarily means ownership."

Last, the items had to be obscene, which meant that the material must "appeal to a reader's or viewer's prurient interest, that is to say, it must have as its dominant purpose and effect erotic allurement, a calculated and effective excitement to sexual desire." The Court applied the test of *Roth v. United States* and *Alberts v. California*, two recent Supreme Court cases decided together in the spring of 1957. *Roth-Alberts* was the Supreme Court's attempt at standardizing obscenity nationwide by creating a three-part test. Prior to *Roth-Alberts* the famous line of Justice Potter Stewart of defining obscenity as "I know it when I see it" had prevailed but was not legally satisfying. Lybarger quoting *Roth-Alberts* said, "The standard for judging obscenity is whether to the average person applying contemporary community standards, the dominate theme of the material, taken as a whole, appeals to prurient interest."

A prophetic statement, in actuality a quite common point, ended Judge Lybarger's jury instructions. "This case is of great importance to the State, and it is of great importance to the defendant, Dollree Mapp." On hindsight he also could have mentioned the case's importance to police officers and would-be defendants all across the United States. He, along with the others, Carl Delau, Michael Haney, Gertrude Mahon, A. L. Kearns, and Dollree Mapp herself, had no idea that that September morning was the beginning and not the end of the legal issues surrounding Dollree Mapp's arrest.

CHAPTER SIX
The Appeal

It seemed to take the jury no time at all. "After due consideration"[1] the jury returned a verdict in favor of the State and against the defendant. Signed by the foreman, Richard J. Kendall, the form, dated September 4, 1958, found "Dollree Mapp Guilty of Possession of Obscene Literature as charged in the indictment."[2] Now a convicted felon, Dollree Mapp faced one to seven years in the Ohio Reformatory for Women and a fine of between $200 and $2000. Although she was sentenced to an indefinite term in the Ohio Reformatory for Women, she never served a day.

Within several days Mapp and her attorney filed a motion for a new trial. Case Number 24699 was filed by A. L. Kearns on behalf of Dollree Mapp in the Court of Appeals for the Eighth Judicial District of Ohio. Her sentence was suspended pending the appeal. The eight reasons given in her appeal for a new trial were plainly and straightforwardly stated.

1. That the verdict of the jury was contrary to the evidence.
2. That Section 2905.34 of the Revised Code of Ohio is unconstitutional.
3. That the defendant was denied her constitutional right of due process of law.
4. That the court erred in overruling the motion to suppress evidence at trial.
5. That the court erred in the admission of evidence offered by the State.

---

[1]   Original trial transcript of *Mapp v. Ohio*, Court of Common Pleas, Criminal Division, p. 118.

[2]   Jury verdict form, C.C. 35 5M 1835-52, Court of Common Pleas, Case No. 36091.

6. That the court erred in not discharging the case when the State rested in trial.

7. That the court erred in not dismissing the case at the close of all evidence.

8. Other errors appearing on the face of the record objected during the course of trial.

Kearns signed his two-page motion, noting his address, 1101 Hippodrome Building, Cleveland 14, Ohio, Main 103543.[3]

Most of Kearns's motion was standard for appeal. However, reasons two through five would later be given teeth. The Ohio statute (cited in reason two) was extremely restrictive, punishing those for mere possession of obscene material. The accused did not have to sell it, buy it, transport it, or manufacture it. Possessing it, not even owning it, was enough to be criminally liable. The statute and its previous interpretation, *State of Ohio v. Lindway*, would come into focus upon appeal. The third, fourth, and fifth reasons, focused on the search and seizure of evidence. While mentioned after the obscenity statute, the search and seizure would prove to be the undoing of the original trial decision. The evidence and the method of obtaining it would be the most interesting aspect to the Supreme Court justices.

Lybarger quickly overruled the motion for new trial. On October 6, 1958, within the thirty-day time limit, Mapp filed a Bill of Exceptions. It was acknowledged as received by the court by David Kikstadt, the deputy clerk to Emil J. Masgay, the clerk of courts. Notice was filed with the county prosecutor, John. T. Corrigan, on October 8, 1958. By October 17th, the Bill

---

[3] Motion for New Trial, Court of Common Pleas, *State of Ohio v. Dollree Mapp, a.k.a. Dolly Mapp.*

of Exception was transmitted to Lybarger, who then, allowed it.[4] The Mapp case would be heard in an appellate court.

By March of 1959 the state of Ohio and Dollree Mapp were in court again, this time in the Court of Appeals of the state of Ohio located in Cuyahoga County. On appeal, Gertrude Mahon concluded that the evidence was clear and convincing that the defendant, Mapp, was knowingly in possession of obscene material. "The jury evidently did not believe her story concerning one Morris Jones."[5] Kearns argued just as directly. He began by stating that the sentence imposed by the state was cruel and unusual. Mapp was a "respectable mother of a 13-year old child" not a shopkeeper who sold obscene items.[6] The typical sentence was a small fine and brief jail term, therefore Mapp's indeterminate sentence of a felony conviction would allow the state to detain her for up to seven years. All the errors at trial, he argued, should have been resolved in favor of Mapp rather than the windfall going to the state. The statute was vague and meaningless and the veil of innocence protected Mapp with such gray evidence.

The appellate court was most interested and concerned about the Ohio statute that made the possession of obscene material, regardless of the reasons for the possession, a felony punishable by fine and/or jail time. The Ohio statute in question became law October 5, 1955. The state of Ohio enacted the law "in the interest of the people and in the interest of the public generally."[7] For Gertrude Mahon, the use of the police powers to protect the health, safety, welfare, and morality of citizens was a justifiable motivation for legislatures to enact statutes such as the Ohio obscenity statute. "The statute is no more unconstitutional or an invalid exercise of the police powers of the state, than would be, for example, the legislation prohibiting the mere possession of a

---

[4]   Original trial transcript of *Mapp v. Ohio*, Court of Common Pleas, Criminal Division, pp. 118-20.

[5]   Court of Appeals, trial transcript, brief of appellee, p. 5.

[6]   Court of Appeals, trial transcript, brief of defendant, pp. 2-8.

[7]   Court of Appeals, trial transcript, brief of appellee, p. 5.

narcotic drug, regardless of the purpose of the possession, that is, whether possession of the drug was for one's own use or for sale."[8] For Kearns, the statute was rare in the United States for both its formulation of a crime and the subsequent punishment. While the method used to seize the material was mentioned, it was the statute itself that was under fire on appeal.

Kearns made mention time and again that the force used by the police was unjustified. His frustration at never actually seeing the search warrant was palpable. "Mrs. Mapp's private home was forced, and then entry sought to be justified by claim of search warrant, never allowed to be seen, let alone read by the defendant, shown to her attorney, or produced in court by the police."[9] Nevertheless he quickly turned his attention to the material seized and Mapp's claim that the obscene items did not belong to her. He noted that the police seized the obscene items along with some items that belonged to Dollree, such as her medical diet list and her mortgage papers. They purposely omitted, he argued, items of Morris Jones that were clearly his, such as books with his name marked clearly across the front. Kearns doubted the intentions of the officers; however, he quickly returned to what he perceived as his strongest legal argument, the state statute.

The statute was cruel, argued Kearns, because it punished both innocent and guilty alike. The old statute, before being amended in 1955, made possession of obscene material only a crime if it was coupled with the purpose of advertising, lending, selling, publishing, or exhibiting. The revised state code made possession alone, for whatever purpose, a felony offense. No matter how innocent the purpose, material deemed obscene violated the state statute. Similar statutes concerning intoxicating liquor, defined possession and the intent associated with it as critical for establishing a crime. Kearns argued that no possession took place using the nexus of the liquor statutes. The items were being stored by Mapp for her boarder but there was no intent to exhibit, sell,

---

[8]   Ibid., p. 5.

[9]   Court of Appeals, transcript, brief of defendant appellant, p. 2.

distribute, and the like. The typical punishment for possessing obscene literature for sale is a fine of $100 or sixty days in jail.[10] The statute therefore violated Article I, Section 9 of the Constitution of the State of Ohio which reads much like the Eighth Amendment of the United States Constitution: "Excessive bail shall not be required; nor excessive fines imposed; nor cruel and unusual punishment inflicted."

It is interesting that no one ever argues that the items seized from the Mapp home were *not* obscene. At trial and on appeal, this strain of argument is never heard. Justice Frankfurter later mused that if these books were obscene, then Mark Twain himself was one of this country's great purveyors of pornography. But this was some two years later. The focus at trial and on appeal was the restrictive nature of the statute. Whether the items that were "merely being possessed" were in fact obscene was never debated. Carl Delau and Mike Haney both indicated that the items were obscene. In recounting the facts years later, Delau turned up his nose and made a face as if he had just encountered something foul and vile. Haney too looked as if he had just drunk rancid milk. Even Dollree Mapp never argued to me that the material seized from her home was not obscene.[11] Thus the quiet consensus of the nature of the items hastened Mapp's guilt. The finer point of "possession" or "under control" did not erase the fact that the items were seen by all as smut. Kearns never made a case to the jury or the appellate court that the books and drawings seized from Dollree Mapp were not obscene and were protected by the First Amendment freedom of expression. It was a given that the material was pornographic.

On March 31, 1959, almost twenty-two months after the search took place, Judge Joy Seth Hurd upheld the trial court and ruled that no error occurred that was prejudicial to the rights of the defendant. Dollree Mapp's punishment was within the purview of the trial court. Affirming Judge Donald Lybarger and the judgment of the Court of Common Pleas, Judge Hurd ordered Dollree Mapp to

---

[10]   Court of Appeals, transcript, p. 18, citing *City of Cincinnati v. King,* 6 O. O. (2d), 313.

[11]   Interviews with Carl Delau 1992, Michael Haney 1992, and Dollree Mapp 1992.

reimburse the state for the costs associated with appeal. She had lost once again. Judge Hurd ordered the Court of Common Pleas to carry out this judgement, meaning in accordance with a guilty finding, carry out the sentence of the convicted.

It appeared Dollree Mapp would go to jail. Yet her legal remedies were not exhausted. The date was March 31, 1959. It would be almost twenty-two more months before it was settled whether or not Dollree Mapp would serve time within the confines of the Women's Reformatory in Ohio.

Mapp filed a motion for appeal with the Supreme Court of Ohio on April 24, 1959. The seven justices of the state Supreme Court comprised the court of last resort within the state of Ohio for Dollree Mapp. She, through her attorney A. L. Kearns, would have to convince the justices that the Ohio statute, Section 2905.34, was unconstitutional for making possession of obscene material a felony, regardless of intent. As will be made clear, the requirement for Mapp to prevail proved even tougher.

Whereas Dollree Mapp had a hard time convincing a jury and appellate court that the lewd material found in her home was not hers, for the Supreme Court of Ohio this fact was irrelevant. Even if there were errors in the trial court in the application of Section 2905.34, the central question the justices focused upon was "whether the constitutional questions raised require a reversal of the judgment under review."[12] The focus was on the interpretation of the terms "possession" and "under control." However, the scope of inquiry broadened to include the search itself. Still not the primary question on appeal, the search of Mapp's home would get more scrutiny by the Supreme Court justices than at any point prior.

The case that would be the most critical to the outcome of the Supreme Court of Ohio's decision was *State of Ohio v. Lindway,*[13] a case turning on the search and seizure conducted by the police. The case of Mike J. Lindway is

---

[12]   Ohio Supreme Court, 166 N.E. 2d 387, 389.
[13]   131 Ohio St. 166.

almost an earlier version of the Mapp case. Also coming from Cuyahoga County, it involved Lieutenant Gloeckner of the Cleveland Police Department and his investigation in 1935 into a series of bombings. A number of nighttime bombings of the homes of employees of a manufacturing company had occurred. Mr. Lindway had once worked for the company as a machinist. Based on information received by the police, Gloeckner and two other officers went to the home of Lindway on March 27, 1935. Mr. Lindway was not present but his wife was confronted by the police. The stories diverge here, Mrs. Lindway claiming the police showed their badge and proceeded to search without hesitation. The police, on the other hand, testified that they advised Mrs. Lindway of the alleged presence of explosives, ammunition, and guns. She denied this and invited them to come in and see for themselves. One point of agreement is that the search of the Lindway home occurred without a search warrant.

The search proved fruitful. The police discovered a loaded .38 revolver, an automatic pistol, ammunition, and a rifle concealed behind the "ice box" (refrigerator). A search of the basement uncovered a locked room with all the equipment to make bombs. Wrapped in newspaper hidden beneath some tools, the police found two bombs, each very sophisticated with a 23 percent nitroglycerine content. Based on the evidence, Mr. Lindway was convicted and sentenced to prison. On appeal, his conviction was reversed, in a two-to-one decision, on the grounds that the trial court erred in overruling the motion to suppress, thus allowing the damning evidence into trial. The search was illegal, argued the two appellate judges, and the evidence against Lindway should be excluded.

In interpreting Article I, Section 14 of the Constitution of the State of Ohio, the majority in *Lindway* reasoned that "an officer of the law who makes a search and seizure in a dwelling or other premises, without a warrant or with an illegal warrant is a trespasser, and amenable to an action for such trespass."[14]

---

[14]   Ohio v. *Lindway*, 131 Ohio St. 166.

The common law belief that a "man's home is his castle" and that the violation was a trespass were common in many other states. But evidence seized illegally was not automatically rendered inadmissible.[15] Under the Constitution and current case law, probative and pertinent evidence would be used against the accused. In other words, Ohio did not utilize the rule of exclusion. Even if the method of seizure proved a violation, the result would not cause the evidence to be excluded. "An application or motion to suppress or exclude such evidence made before trial or during trial is properly denied. The court need not concern itself with the collateral issue of how the evidence was procured."[16]

Ohio v. Lindway is a classic example of the state of search and seizure law before *Mapp v. Ohio* reached the Supreme Court of the United States. Ohio, like many states, considered the quality of the evidence over the quality of the search that procured it. In *Ohio v. Lindway*, the Supreme Court of Ohio reversed the appeals court, allowing the evidence to be admitted. The court noted that the Fourth Amendment to the United States Constitution is directed

exclusively against the activities of the federal government and has no application to the various states and their agencies. However, most state constitutions, including that of Ohio, contain identical or similar provisions, and the decisions are in general agreement that searches and seizures are unreasonable and illegal in the absence of a valid warrant. Therefore, a law officer who proceeds to make a search and seizure without a warrant, or under a defective warrant, is a trespasser, amenable to civil and perhaps criminal action.[17]

---

[15] This commonality was at the heart of Justice Frankfurter's opinion in *Wolf v. Colorado* (1949). The number of states with statutes and constitutions such as Ohio's convinced Frankfurter that states provided an adequate remedy for search and seizure violations and that the exclusionary rule was not mandatory.

[16] From the syllabus of *Ohio v. Lindway*, 131 Ohio St. 166, also citing the fifth paragraph of the syllabus of *Nicholas v. City of Cleveland*, 125 Ohio St. 474 and *Browning v. City of Cleveland*, 126 Ohio St. 285.

[17] *Ohio v. Lindway*, 131 Ohio St. 166.

The remedy, however, is not exclusion, at least not in 1959. The *Lindway* case reads like *Wolf v. Colorado*, supportive of the idea of allowing each state to tailor its police misconduct problems with solutions that meet the needs of their citizenry. The court noted that some states, along with the federal government, support the idea that courts should not receive evidence that has been secured illegally because its admission is "tantamount to compelling an accused to be a witness against himself, and their exclusion presents the most practical methods of enforcing the guarantee against unreasonable searches and seizures."[18] However these states are not in the majority. Most, the court noted, hold that if the evidence is probative and sheds light on the guilt or innocent of the accused, then courts need not concern themselves with the collateral issue of how it was obtained. Still further, "the people of the state ought not to be penalized by the suppression of evidence tending to prove an offense against the peace and dignity of the state to shield a criminal from deserved punishment, when the Constitution by its plain language makes no such demand."[19] The court continued with the litany of cases supporting this legal logic, from *Boyd v. United States* to *Wolf v. Colorado*. Next the justices presented state decisions that supported different treatment of the search and the items seized. The case law indicated a tendency to favor the securing of a warrant and split on the use of evidence if one was not obtained or requested. "Because of the uncertainty existing in our own decisions and because of conflicting decisions in the lower courts of this state, it would seem both wise and necessary to lay down a definite rule unqualifiedly aligning ourselves with either the "admissionists" or "exclusionists."[20]

While it was not clear by past cases and looking nationally for trends whether the evidence seized against Mike Lindway should be used by the court at trial, the Supreme Court of Ohio decided that illegally obtained evidence

---

18   Ibid.

19   Ibid.

20   Ibid.

should not be excluded from use at trial. The question of the legality of the search was not the focal point. The focus was the evidence itself and its probative value. The Supreme Court of Ohio reversed the Court of Appeals, thereby affirming the Court of Common Pleas decision. An illegal search, while compounding the problems confronting a trial court, did not derail the use of evidence at trial.

The problem with excluding evidence was highlighted in the majority opinion. Quoting the well-known text *Evidence*, the opinion read: "All this is misguided sentimentality. For the sake of indirectly and contingently protecting the Fourth Amendment, this view appears indifferent to the direct and immediate result of making Justice inefficient, and of coddling the criminal classes of the population. It puts Supreme Courts in the position of assisting to undermine the foundations of the very institutions they are set there to protect. It regards the over zealous officer of the law as a greater danger to the community than the unpunished murderer or embezzler or panderer."[21] The court went even further. "And to bring the list more up to date we might add the terms gangster, gunman, racketeer and kidnaper."[22] The very essence of the argument against the exclusionary rule was laid out. An illegal search was problematic. The solution, however, was not to throw the evidence out.

Mapp v. Ohio, decided by the Supreme Court of the United States in 1961 would change all that. But for now, in the spring of 1959, *Lindway* and its impact on *Mapp v. Ohio* in the Supreme Court of the State of Ohio was a different matter. *Lindway* was crucial to the decision in the *Mapp* case. Yet, the primary focus was still on section 2905.34.

It was clear that the search itself was becoming more of a problem for Gertrude Mahon. Never producing the warrant cast a shadow on the legality of the search. Justice Taft summed up the warrant issue plainly.

---

[21]   Ibid., quoting John Henry Wigmore, *Evidence, Evidence in Trial at Common Law* 2nd ed., vol. 4, p. 637.

[22]   *Ohio v. Lindway*, 131 Ohio St. 166, 181.

There is, in the record, considerable doubt as to whether there ever was any warrant for the search of defendant's home. No warrant was offered in evidence, there was no testimony as to who issued any warrant or as to what any warrant contained, and the absence from evidence of any such warrant is not explained or otherwise accounted for in the record. Admittedly therefore there was no warrant authorizing a search of defendant's home for any "lewd, or lascivious book, print, [or] picture."[23]

However, relying on *Lindway*, it did not make a difference. "This court has held that evidence obtained by an unlawful search and seizure is admissible in a criminal prosecution."[24] The search of Dollree Mapp's home was unlawful, said the court, but that fact did not justify the exclusion of the obscene items as evidence in her trial.

The remainder of the Ohio Supreme Court decision concerned Section 2905.34. Problematic is the finding of guilt by mere possession of obscene material. Most state laws forbid the possession if it is for the purpose of selling, lending, or exhibiting. The Ohio statute forbids the possession of obscene items *per se*, even if innocently acquired. Such a statute, reasoned the majority, would discourage otherwise law abiding citizens from even looking at books or pictures and thereby abridges their First Amendment rights of freedom of speech and press. Judges Taft, Peck, Zimmerman, Matthias, and Weygandt held that the Ohio statute was unconstitutional and the judgment of the Court of Appeals should be reversed.[25] It would appear that Dollree Mapp's conviction would be overturned because of the restrictive nature of the Ohio statute.

However, the Constitution of Ohio stipulated that in order for the judiciary to negate a state law, all but one judge must agree unless the Court of Appeals too agrees that the statute was unconstitutional.[26] The lower court had supported the state statute and only five judges, not six of the Supreme Court members, felt that Section 2905.34 should be voided. Dollree Mapp was one

---

[23]   Ibid.

[24]   Ibid.

[25]   Ibid.

[26]   Constitution of the State of Ohio, Article IV, Section 2.

vote short. "Since more than one of the judges [Herbert and Bell] of this court are of the opinion that no portion of the statute upon which defendant's conviction was based is unconstitutional and void, the judgement of the Court of Appeals must be affirmed."[27]

What a devastating blow the majority opinion must have been to Dollree Mapp and her attorney. The search was illegal, but no matter; the evidence could be used against her. The statute which made the seized evidence a felony was declared unconstitutional by five of the seven justices on the highest bench in Ohio but the margin of victory was not enough to overturn her conviction. She had come so close to victory, but the conviction of the Court of Common Pleas still held. Dollree Mapp was guilty and faced an indeterminate time in prison, up to seven years.

The Supreme Court dealt a blow as well to the Cleveland Police Department and Officers Delau, Haney, and Dever. The search was illegal. The failure to ever produce a search warrant was suspicious. Justice Herbert in dissent argued that this case affords "a perfect opportunity for the court to modify and limit the Lindway rule" and create a more reasonable interpretation of the state constitution's search and seizure provision.[28] Herbert's argument dealt not merely with the search and seizure of Mapp but also linked that legal question with the earlier question of possession of obscene material. Just as he suggests a revisitation of *Lindway*, so would United States Supreme Court Associate Justice Tom Clark suggest a revisiting of *Wolf v. Colorado*. If, Herbert argued, it could be shown that Mapp intended to sell or print the obscene materials, the case would be very different. Noting that a printing press was not found or a volume of copies that indicated the intent to sell, the search was less justified. In other words, search and seizure violations were justified by the egregiousness of what was found. He quoted often the concurrence of

---

[27]   166 N. E. 2d 387, 434.

[28]   Ibid. Article I, Section 14 of the Ohio Constitution is a verbatim recitation of the Fourth Amendment of the United States.

Justice Jones in *Lindway* who condemned the search but allowed it because it produced such hard evidence of a serious crime. Herbert, as well as his colleagues, were still not willing to agree that a search and seizure violation resulted in exclusion, regardless of the probative value of the evidence. Mapp possessed pornography with no evidence to suggest that she was a distributor or manufacturer of it. The violation posed a harm because "it was not the class of criminal element alluded to but the class embodying millions of citizens who are innocent of any offense or whose offenses are minor. The decision of this court in the instant case is too broad, since it is made to apply to everyone suspected of committing any offense whatever."[29] Using what will later be termed a cost-benefit analysis, Justices Bell and Herbert felt that Mapp's offense was minor, therefore the *Lindway* argument of Jones would dictate that the evidence against her be excluded. This was little consolation to Dollree Mapp. She had lost again, however the Supreme Court of Ohio had opened the door of doubt. The grounds for appeal were laid on March 23, 1960, when the Supreme Court of the State of Ohio, in a five to two vote, affirmed the lower court decision in spite of commentary that left both the search itself and the obscenity statute weakened and suspect.

---

[29]   Quoting Justice Jones concurrence in *Lindway*, 166 N.E. 2d, 387, 394.

CHAPTER SEVEN
The Supreme Court of the United States

Three months after the Supreme Court of Ohio's decision was issued, June 15, 1960, Walter L. Green gave notice of appeal in criminal case number 36091. He raised six questions for review by the Supreme Court of the United States. The first two asked the Court to decide if the Ohio obscenity statute was unconstitutional. This had been Kearns's and Green's original complaint before the Court of Common Pleas of Cuyahoga County. The third and fourth raised the questions of whether or not the sentence Mapp received was cruel and unusual. The last questions concerned the lack of review of the sentence by the Court of Appeals and State Supreme Court and the manner and content of charges made to the jury. The fifth question, whether it was placed in the list by order of importance or randomly, addressed the legal problems resulting from the conduct of the police. "Did the conduct of the police in procuring the books, papers and pictures placed in evidence by the Prosecution violate Amendment IV, Amendment V, and Amendment XIV Section 1 of the United States Constitution; and Article I Section 1, and Article I Section 14 of the Ohio Constitution?"[1] Appeals typically include each and every grievance possible in hopes that the totality of the argument may strengthen the validity of the most persuasive ones. Widening the scope of a court's purview always comes with risk. Would the best arguments be obscured by the volume of complaints? Would the power of a singular well-stated argument be diminished

---

[1] Notice of Appeal to the Supreme Court of the United States, *The State of Ohio vs. Dollree Mapp.*

by the multitude of grievances? A. L. Kearns and Walter Green most likely wrote their appeal with the more egregious errors stated first and foremost. The Ohio Supreme Court's focus on the obscenity statute and the resulting split decision was, from their point of view, the best legal argument to set forth before the high court.

Seven months after the decision of the Supreme Court of Ohio, the Supreme Court of the United States noted probable jurisdiction in the case of *Mapp v. Ohio*. The date was October 24, 1960. With little fanfare it was evaluated by the law clerks within each of the justices' chambers. Justice Clark's clerk, Carl Estes II, drafted a three-page note setting forth the grounds for jurisdictional control of *Mapp v. Ohio*. Most of his memorandum focused on the obscenity statute. His only mention of the search and seizure indicated that despite Mapp's claim of an illegal search, the Ohio law did not appear to breach the *Rochin* standard.[2] Warren's clerk also recommended taking the case, claiming the grounds of which were solely based on the First Amendment. The argument that Mapp was a victim of an illegal search was irrelevant, since Ohio law was applied correctly and consistently with *Wolf v. Colorado*.[3] The issue seemed clear. In light of the *Lindway* case, did the state of Ohio have the right to punish those who merely possess materials deemed obscene?

In revisiting the memos and writings of clerks and justices, it appeared to be viewed by all of them as an obscenity case. It raised fundamental questions of privacy, of censorship. Gearing up for this intellectual debate meant revisiting the classic tradeoffs of a free society; individual tastes and preferences of expression versus state control, on behalf of the health, safety, welfare, and morality of its citizens. The method of obtaining the materials in

---

[2]   See Box B178, Folder 5, Tom C. Clark Papers, Tarlton Law Library, The University of Texas at Austin, Austin, Texas.

[3]   See Box 210, File Petition for rehearing/conference memos/bench memos, Earl Warren Papers, Library of Congress, Manuscript Room, Washington, D.C.

question loomed in the background. The nagging legal quandary seemed to focus on the strict Ohio statute.

However, not everyone saw the First Amendment issues as paramount. In February 1961, Bernard Berkman of the Cleveland branch of the American Civil Liberties Union filed an amicus curiae, or friend of the court brief, in docket number 236. In it he argued that the central issue in the case was not what Dolly Mapp possessed but how the police came to seize those possessions. Berkman argued in simple and direct language that Mapp's Fourth Amendment rights were violated. He stated clearly, with an eye on the Fourth Amendment, that she was a victim of an illegal search and seizure. The ACLU amicus brief was only two paragraphs long. Berkman did not advocate or present a rationale for his conclusions. He stated what he saw as obvious: the search of Dollree Mapp's home was unreasonable and therefore violated the Fourth Amendment of the United States Constitution.

Timing mattered. Although the case of *Mapp v. Ohio* was accepted for review by the Supreme Court of the United States in the fall of 1960, this might not have been so if it had come at a different time in the doctrinal development of the Constitution. Perhaps the Court would have still taken the case. I doubt it. Even if the justices did decide to address the issues raised in *Mapp v. Ohio*, it is likely the outcome would have been quite different from the status quo. But decades of indecisions that led up to *Mapp v. Ohio* made the legal questions raised by this case even more relevant to a Court that now seemed inclined to change the law. The issues raised were salient. The Fourth Amendment quandary came before the right nine justices at a particular point in their legal development. Clearly questions surrounding searches and seizures were more important for resolution for some of the justices, as we shall see. Remember, too, that for all intents, *Mapp v. Ohio* was taken for review on First Amendment grounds, not Fourth. So a ripe constitutional claim came to the Court under the guise of a freedom of expression issue, the more salient Fourth Amendment question merely a subtext.

~~~

To appreciate the intersection of the legal questions involved in *Mapp v. Ohio* and the justices who answered them, one must step back in time to understand the Court's focus. The Court's docket was changing, moving to one that included more cases involving attempts to curtail crime. These alterations to the docket reflect a sense of urgency in confronting these issues. America had experienced a surge in the crime rate in the late 1920s, fostering a focus in the 1930s on controlling crime. Prohibition, the growth of organized crime, and the concern for the breakdown of law and order in the face of the Great Depression, led to a more professionalized and energized Federal Bureau of Investigation. With J. Edgar Hoover at the helm, the FBI became an imposing agency, the leader in law enforcement.

Congress also did its part to toughen up the approach to crime. They passed the Lindbergh Law in June of 1932, making kidnaping a federal offense when the victim is transported across state lines. Also enacted were a number of other federal statutes placing more crimes under the scope of federal authority. The first wiretapping legislation was passed in 1934. In 1935-36 the federal government even advocated universal fingerprinting of all Americans, so intent was the government on curbing serious crime. This idea was popular for several years but eventually fell into disfavor.[4] The judiciary found its docket expanding to accommodate the questions that inevitably arise from such a concerted policy agenda.

By the 1940s the country and the institutions of government were focused more on the war abroad than on domestic problems. Crime took a backstage to the war in Europe. However, by 1945, post–World War II America again experienced a sharp increase in the rate of crime. Racial tension surged as black service members, returning from fighting the racism of the Nazis, ironically

---

[4]   Samuel Walker, *Popular Justice: A History of American Criminal Justice* (New York: Oxford University Press, 1980), pp. 184-88.

and tragically experienced discrimination at home. FBI Director Hoover's concern of communist infiltration during the Cold War led to witch hunts. Exposing those who sympathized with the enemy was paramount. The reaction by many cities was to get tough on crime. Crime fighters such as Los Angeles Police Chief William Parker declared a "war on crime" much to the dismay of the targets of such policy: poor blacks and Latinos.

The 1950s found the country divided by the questions of race and equality. The Civil Rights Movement raised the consciousness of many about the rights of those who were poor and oppressed. By the early 1960s, this struggle for equality not only included racial minorities but societal minorities, including even criminals. The balance between controlling crime and affording rights to those accused of committing crimes polarized the country. Gallup polls regularly reported that Americans were fearful of crime and saw it as one of the most important problems facing government.

The judiciary was not immune to such social changes. The Great Depression found the Court initially unsupportive of the Roosevelt recovery program. The famous "hundred days" legislation of Roosevelt found a hostile Court in the cases of *Carter v. Carter Coal Company,*[5] *Schecter Poultry Company v. United States,*[6] and *United States v. Butler,*[7] President Roosevelt's court-packing plan quickly put the justices on the defensive. The Roosevelt agenda, overwhelmingly supported by the electorate and its representatives, lacked only the support of the third branch of government to complete the social architecture of change.

The White House proposed a plan to reorganize the Supreme Court in order to assist the aging justices with their workload. The headlines of the *New York Times* on February 6, 1937, screamed, "*ROOSEVELT ASKS POWER TO REFORM COURTS, INCREASING THE SUPREME BENCH TO 15*

---

[5]   298 U.S. 238 (1936).

[6]   295 U.S. 495 (1935).

[7]   297 U.S. 1 (1936).

JUSTICES; CONGRESS STARTLED, BUT EXPECTED TO APPROVE."[8]
Roosevelt eventually lost his bid to alter the size of the Supreme Court, but he
won the battle overall. A rapid and undeniable "switch in time saved the nine."
Within a year of the introduction of the Court Reorganization Act, the justices
upheld the administration's alterations to bolster the American economy. Two
justices switched in cases such as *National Labor Relations Board v. Jones and
Laughlin Steel Corp.*[9] and *West Coast Hotel v. Parrish*,[10] which affirmed the
Roosevelt agenda. The lesson for the justices was to carve out issue areas that
were less likely to result in combative altercations with congress and the
president. Their docket reflected this change. No longer would the core of the
Court's workload be economic cases but cases of individual rights and liberties.

Cases of liberty versus authority now comprised the bread and butter of the
judiciary. Balancing the rights of the accused against the need for the safety and
security of society were a staple. The Court moved rapidly from the concern for
crime control to focusing on civil rights and due process. Scholars would later
label this pendulum swing, this change of focus, the "due process revolution."
Cases involving individual rights for criminals were supported by the growing
liberal alliance on the Court, with the compliance of at least one of the more
moderate justices. Change was the order of the day. It was evident in the
concerns of Americans, of lawmakers, and of the Court. Postwar America
looked very different than the interwar America of Prohibition and organized
crime. Equality and fairness had moved to the forefront. Thus began "the most
profound and pervasive revolution ever achieved by substantially peaceful
means."[11] The rights revolution, rooted in the societal divisions of the
Depression, fueled by war and the heightened need for security, and
culminating in the polar divisions of black and white, rich and poor, communist

---

[8]   *New York Times*, February 6, 1937, p.A1.

[9]   301 U.S. 1 (1937).

[10]   300 U.S. 379 (1937).

[11]   Justice Abe Fortas as quoted in Bernard Schwartz's *Super Chief: Earl Warren and His
       Supreme Court* (New York: New York University Press, 1983), p. 48.

and patriot, became the catalyst for judicial action. The rule of law was to become the tool of change. Those wielding the tool were the justices of the Warren Court.

The Warren Court's rights revolution, in terms of the rights of the accused, reached its zenith in the 1960s, but clearly the foundation of revolution was established much earlier. While the police were investigating the numbers war in Cleveland, and while Dollree Mapp was soon to encounter the police again, court watchers from Eisenhower on down labeled the Supreme Court as coddling criminals and "soft" on crime. Protecting the liberties of this minority of law violators was unpopular. By the end of Warren's tenure, the Court would be severely criticized for being a super legislature, for going beyond the scope of the institution, and for changing the very fabric of American society. Those changes would later be heralded as part of the democratization of America, but only in hindsight.

For Earl Warren, the turning point in the treatment of those accused of crimes by the state came earlier than *Mapp v. Ohio*. Warren had served as a county prosecutor in Alameda County, as attorney general of a large state (California), and even as governor. With only a brief period in private legal practice, Earl Warren had served the public, often in a law enforcement capacity. While he was aware of police abuse and the fight against it, Warren's understanding of the problem of governmental abuse in police-citizen relations took on a new light with his new job as a Supreme Court justice. Warren's arrival at the Supreme Court in 1953 as chief justice found him learning from those with experience. Having never donned a judicial robe, Warren allowed Justice Hugo Black, who had been on the Court since 1937, to lead the secret conferences of the justices. Warren's prior political experience brought an understanding of the issues, but the role of judge gave him a fresh perspective on issues he had always considered in a different light. His lack of judicial experience, while initially met with criticism, may in some ways have proven to be one of his greatest assets.

A watershed case in his judicial understanding of the relationship between citizens and their government was *Irvine v. California.*[12] The case concerned the treatment of Patrick Irvine by the Long Beach Police Department. Suspecting that Irvine was involved in illegal gambling, the police wiretapped his home. The level of intrusion into Irvine's private life was unprecedented. The police locksmith first made a key of Irvine's front door without his knowledge. Then the police used it to illegally enter his home numerous times to install electronic eavesdropping equipment. Recording engineers bored holes in the walls and even the roof of Irvine's home to conceal numerous listening devices. Over a thirty-day period the police entered Irvine's home on several occasions, never once obtaining a search warrant. The fruits of their efforts were enough to convict him on the charges of bookmaking.

When the case reached the Supreme Court in 1954, there was little doubt that Irvine's rights were violated. Some of the Justices, including Warren, were incensed by the flagrant violation. Warren's bench memo reflects his distaste for the police action. He recalls the numerous entries by the police.

> Later, after a little experience with the device (the wiretap), the police were not pleased with the job they had done. They couldn't hear enough. The electrician was recalled; he and the officers reentered the "locked" house and relocated the microphone. The police still weren't satisfied. For a third time the electrician was recalled; there was more tampering with the fixtures, more ransacking of the house to find the best location.[13]

The statements seized as a result of the police activity were admitted into evidence against Irvine. Irvine objected, citing his Fourth Amendment rights, quoting from *Rochin v. California*[14] that the police misconduct "shocks the

---

[12]   *Irvine v. California*, 347 U.S. 128 (1954).

[13]   Bench memo of *Irvine v. California*, Box 152, Earl Warren Papers, Library of Congress, Manuscript Room, Washington, D.C.

[14]   342 U.S. 165.

conscience" as an affront to due process and fairness. His objection was overruled, the evidence was admitted, and Irvine was subsequently convicted.

Such a result did not sit well with Warren. Despite his background as a district attorney and attorney general, Warren felt that

> we have, what seems to me a most flagrant violation of the home and of personal privacy and of the 14th Amendment. Petitioner may have been a bookie and an unsavory character, but he owned the house which the police invaded. It was his home, and the invasion was a forcible and patent trespass—if not a crime. This, I think, was more than a trespass against property; it was a trespass against the person.[15]

Common law logic aside, Warren quickly moved on to the more crucial point. An addendum to his bench memo, written in longhand, reasons, "There is no doubt of it—there was an illegal invasion. But must there be a reversal of it?" His answer: "I think not."[16]

The result Earl Warren reaches is somewhat surprising. Perhaps he was not fully settled in his role as jurist and viewed the facts from the vantage point he had held most of his public life. He reasoned that the Court could take into consideration the actions of the state as distinguished from the "blundering constable" of Mr. Cardozo.[17] The state ruled the wiretap illegal and held the errant police officers legally liable for their actions. Going still further to exclude the evidence against Irvine, using the logic of *Wolf v. Colorado* was not necessary.[18] The Court thereby noted the illegal activity of the police but felt uneasy losing the evidence altogether.

Warren provided the crucial fifth vote allowing the evidence seized against Irvine to be used against him. Justice Jackson's majority view reasoned that the police misconduct, while offensive, did fall under the broad scope of state

---

[15]   Bench memo of *Irvine v. California*.

[16]   Ibid.

[17]   A reference to then Judge Benjamin Nathan Cardozo in *People v. Defore*, 242 N.Y. 13 (1926) stating, "the criminal will go free because the constable has blundered."

[18]   Bench memo of *Irvine v. California*.

authority to set rules of evidence a la *Wolf.* Along with Justices Reed and Minton, the plurality was joined by Justice Tom Clark, who wrote a concurrence. Clark, whose role in the Mapp decision will prove strikingly similar to his role in Irvine, felt that Wolf should be overruled. Yet, if the Court stopped short of such action, he would vote to affirm. In other words, Clark would not join a partial remedy. The right must be met with a remedy. Fourth Amendment violations were either protected through applying the exclusionary rule uniformly or leaving it entirely up to the state. Clark did not want to create a case-by-case exception for extreme violations such as in *Irvine. Rochin,* penned by Frankfurter, had argued such an exception, citing the extreme mistreatment in that case met with the test of "shocking the conscience." Clark's judicial philosophy was undergirded with patience. If the Fourth Amendment right was extended to all by *Weeks v. United States,* then the remedy should also apply uniformly rather than allowing states through *Wolf* to choose its remedial path. This caught the ire of the prickly Frankfurter, who penned a lengthy letter to Clark on December 29, 1953.

"Your position, as I understood it, was that you are prepared to overrule *Wolf v. Colorado,* but if that is not to be done then you would apply Wolf. Will you not agree that Irvine is not precisely *Wolf?*" *Wolf* stated only that state convictions are not invalid because some state evidence would be excluded under federal courts using the exclusionary rule of the Fourth Amendment. But to generalize beyond that strict interpretation extends *Wolf* beyond its original iteration. "Because I do not want to overrule Wolf does not require me to extend it. I know there are some Catholics who are more Catholic than the Pope. You do not have to be more *Wolfish* than *Wolf.*"[19]

Tom Clark made plain in his *Irvine* concurrence in 1954 what he would say in his majority opinion for the Court in *Mapp v. Ohio* in 1961. He begins his opinion in *Irvine,* "Had I been here in 1949 when Wolf was decided I would

---

[19]   Part III, Reel No. 1, pp. 334-35, Papers of Felix Frankfurter, Harvard Law School Collection.

have applied the doctrine of *Weeks v. United States* to the states."[20] In conclusion, Clark seems to lay out his strategy for the future: "In light of the "incredible" activity of the police here it is with great reluctance that I follow *Wolf*. Perhaps strict adherence to the tenor of that decision may bring needed converts to the cause for its extinction. Thus I merely concur in the judgment of affirmance."[21] Converts indeed. The foreshadowing of what was to come was boldly plain. If he could muster the votes, Clark would assert the exclusionary rule as a remedy for Fourth Amendment violations.

The dissenters, Black, Frankfurter, Burton, and Douglas were outraged that the police conduct would go unchecked by the high court. "The search and seizure conducted in this case smack of the police state, not the free America the Bill of Rights envisaged."[22] The majority, it appeared, was also bothered by the actions of the police, but in deference to state law decided against interfering. The holding of *Irvine*, allowing the infringement of Irvine's right on the belief that the remedy lay elsewhere, is an anathema to the collective jurisprudence of the chief justice. Years later, upon reflection, Warren said of his *Irvine* decision, that if there was any vote he could recast in his tenure on the Court, it would be the one in *Irvine v. California*.[23]

The regret about *Irvine* may not have been simply over just the Court's decision. In the aftermath of the litigation, Warren and Jackson had asked that the clerk of the court forward a copy of the case and record to the attorney general of the United States, Herbert Brownell. Warren believed that an investigation by Brownell into the flagrant police misconduct in *Irvine* would result in disciplinary action, even prosecution of the errant police officers. However, no investigation or prosecution ever took place. Warren told his law

---

20   Concurring opinion, J. Clark in *Irvine v. California*, circulated memo February 4, 1954 from Tom Clark to Earl Warren, Box 420, Earl Warren Papers, Library of Congress, Manuscript Room, Washington, D.C.

21   Ibid.

22   347 U.S. 128, at 149.

23   See the address of Edward Bennett Williams, 64 *Cal. L.Rev.* 8 (1976).

clerks of his request and lamented that the Department of Justice had failed to act. One of Warren's clerks stated: "I don't know how the Chief found that out but I assume he may just have asked Brownell what had come of it. And I think that case was a kind of symbol for the Chief."[24]

Herein lies the education of Earl Warren. *Irvine* undoubtedly contributed to the belief by the Chief that justice was not always realized by the Court's decisions. The judiciary could not enforce its own decisions, and belief that other branches of government would carry out the Court's wishes in that regard was possibly misplaced. The role of jurist was different than that of an elected post. But for Warren, the failure to act by others was part of the new reality of his role of jurist. *Irvine* and other cases clearly contributed to Warren's philosophical broadening of the judicial role to include relief that was not being provided elsewhere. Justice had not been served by the decision in *Irvine*, nor by the indecision of the attorney general. The lesson of *Irvine* would stay with Warren and undoubtedly affected his view of search and seizure law and the police. A more active role in interpreting and enforcing constitutional principles was seemingly more necessary. The setting of the stage for the case of *Mapp v. Ohio* was almost complete.

~~~

The nine justices of the Mapp court contained a fascinating group of jurists. Most notable were the powerhouse intellectuals: Justices Frankfurter, Black, and Douglas. Known for both their personal as well as political skills were Chief Justice Warren and William Brennan. Justices Harlan and Clark were prominent and respected, as was Justice Potter Stewart. Least known yet able was Justice Charles Whittaker. These nine men combined the right mix of intellect, politics, social conscience, liberalism, and conservatism. The clashes among them were frequent, since the questions coming before the Court were

---

[24]   Schwartz, *Super Chief,* p. 137.

contentious. The personalities and characters of the nine would combine and ignite. The superlegislature of the Warren era was driven by the Court personnel and the country itself, searching for answers to volatile yet highly relevant questions of the day.

Ascending as the Chief Justice of the highest court in the land on September 30, 1953, Earl Warren quickly found his voice among a court full of highly talented and vocal jurists. The Warren Court was a collection of some of the institution's most capable and strong-willed members. Yale Law Professor Fred Rodell labeled the Court "the most brilliant and able collection of Justices who ever graced the high bench together."[25] Any law student or Court watcher knows the names of Frankfurter, Black, Brennan, Harlan. Even the lesser-known members of Warren's Court were strong, capable, and well accomplished.

The senior statesman of the Court was Hugo Lafayette Black. Born and raised in Alabama, Black was the first appointment to the Supreme Court by President Franklin Delano Roosevelt in 1937. Black's appointment to the high bench was briefly marred by his past. As a young man from 1923 to 1935, Black held membership in the Ku Klux Klan. The controversy stemmed more from the timing of the news of Black's association rather than the association itself. After his Senate confirmation, the national media reported Black's membership so widely that the newly appointed justice explained his membership and subsequent resignation from the Klan on national radio. Black's Senate years highlighted his allegiance to FDR. He spoke out and supported Roosevelt's New Deal programs and agreed with the famous court-packing plan of 1936-1937. His overall record as a Senator prevailed and the controversy over his youthful association subsided.

Black's leadership on the Court was not simply based on longevity. His southern drawl, droopy posture, and slight frame made it easy for others to

---

[25]   Fred Rodell, *Nine Men: A Political History of the Supreme Court from 1790 to 1955* (New York: William S. Hein and Co. 1988). p. 284.

underestimate him. Opponents, legal or otherwise, quickly found out this was a mistake. His intellectual tenacity spilled over to other facets of his life. Black was a competitive tennis player whose devotion to the game was legendary. Even in retirement Black played several sets of tennis per day, causing retired Justice Minton to say, "The Chief calls me up once in a while and gives me a report on you and your tennis game. What a man! I can barely get around on crutches."[26]

Another Roosevelt appointee, one who was different from Hugo Black in almost every way possible was Felix Frankfurter. Born in Vienna, Austria, Frankfurter arrived in the United States with his parents in 1894, making his home in New York. His intellectual skills quickly carried him to Harvard Law School, where he excelled. He became a member of the Jewish elite of Boston, involving himself in the Zionist movement. He regularly socialized and exchanged ideas with leading legal intellectuals such as Learned Hand, Benjamin Cardozo, Louis Brandeis, and Oliver Wendell Holmes, Jr. An original founder of the American Civil Liberties Union, Frankfurter was well known for his outspoken defense of Sacco and Vanzetti in the famous treason trial in 1921. Frankfurter met Franklin Roosevelt when the future president was assistant secretary of the Navy. In 1939, Roosevelt, after asking Frankfurter to serve as solicitor general, a job he declined, asked him to be his third appointee to the high bench. Frankfurter remained an associate justice until August 28, 1962, just months after the *Mapp* decision was handed down and just prior to his eightieth birthday.

Of the nine justices, Frankfurter was the least capable of separating his professional position from personal opinion. He was a legal giant but an intellectual snob. His legal arguments, while sound, were in the end diminished by his lack of respect for those who disagreed with him. He cajoled and belittled the opinions of others who failed to adopt the logic that he so

---

26   Letter dated September 11, 1964, from Sherman Minton to Hugo Black. Papers of Hugo Black, Library of Congress, Manuscript Room, Washington, D.C.

eloquently set forth; indeed the fact that lesser mortals inhabited the Court was unfortunate. Frankfurter's correspondence is full of criticism for his colleagues. For example, in correspondence to his colleague John Marshall Harlan, Frankfurter criticizes Warren's behavior concerning the Little Rock desegregation crisis. He writes,

> I am bound to say that Butler's advice to his School Board was much wiser than the views which Bill Brennan tells me the Chief Justice expressed to you fellows at luncheon last Friday. Of course (Governor) Faubus has been guilty of trickery, but the trickery was as much against the School Board as against us. And in any event the fight is not between the Supreme Court and Faubus, tho apparently that is the way it lay in the C.J.'s mind. I am afraid his attitude toward the kind of problems that confront us are more like that of a fighting politician than that of a judicial statesman. I shudder to think what would have happened to the institution if he had been in Hughes's place at the time that F.D.R. threw down the gage of battle.[27]

The lines between legal reasoning in a professional setting and personal accord were often blurred. No doubt Felix Frankfurter is one of the greatest justices to ever serve on the Supreme Court, but one wonders if his impact could have been greater if he had more tolerance for his colleagues and their differing points of view.

Another intellectual giant with shortcomings of personality was William O. Douglas. Douglas, a liberal who studied at Columbia Law School, was one of the original architects of the Securities and Exchange Commission, serving as chairman in 1937. He was an early environmentalist, known for having helped saved the C&O Canal. His lifelong love of the outdoors stemmed from overcoming polio in his youth. He could be witty and acerbic at the same time. He was persnickety. For example, he penned a memo to the Chief that one of his secretaries is "slowly going blind because of poor lighting." He even

---

[27] Internal memo between Justice Felix Frankfurter and Justice John Marshall Harlan, September 2, 1958, Reel 1, Part III, p 598-99. Felix Frankfurter Papers, Harvard Law School Collection.

advocated the creation of an escort service because a young female summer intern had to make her way alone when a guard refused to walk her to her car late one evening.[28] Ever the supporter of the underdog, Douglas, who began his lengthy court service in 1939, felt the need and duty to right the wrong, however small. For example, he wrote a terse letter to the Chief about his parking pass not being honored at National Airport. After his health deteriorated as a result of a stroke, Douglas wrote a memo to the Chief about the need for a whirlpool for his physical therapy. He insinuated that the Court should buy this for him so that he did not have to travel back and forth to Walter Reed Army Hospital and could therefore better serve the Court by receiving his treatment in-house.[29] On court business Douglas made his decisions with little concern of persuading or co-opting others. His sense was that the law was right and his job was to say so.

The last of the "Mapp Court" to arrive in Washington prior to Warren was Tom Clark from Texas. Clark advocated a philosophy of pragmatism and adherence to the rule of law. This pragmatism would prove crucial to the outcome of *Mapp v. Ohio*. Clark believed in obedience to the law and that cases should be only explicitly overruled, not overruled by implication. He believed it was within his right to dissent during the time in which the Court had jurisdiction over a case, but once the case was decided, the decision should be supported until the time that a coalition was formulated large enough to overturn it. This philosophy can be seen in his comments made in *Irvine v. California* concerning the reach of *Wolf v. Colorado*. This point of view was in play when *Mapp* came to the court, since Clark had watched *Wolf* with dismay and only acted when he had a clear majority to change the law.

Several of the remaining justices who all arrived after Warren, while important to the dynamics of the Court, were less important in the inner

---

[28]   "Correspondence with WOD," Box 351, Earl Warren Papers, Library of Congress, Manuscript Room, Washington, D.C.

[29]   "Correspondence with WOD," memo dated 1965, Box 351, Earl Warren Papers, Library of Congress, Manuscript Room, Washington, D.C.

workings of *Mapp v. Ohio*. Charles Whittaker was nominated by Eisenhower to the high bench on March 2, 1957. He served on the Court only five years. His beginnings were humble, growing up in rural Kansas. Despite this, he rose to become a District Court judge and Eighth Circuit Court judge. Upon the advice of his doctor, Whittaker resigned due to physical exhaustion. He did not return to legal practice or public service.

John Marshall Harlan, intellectual and cerebral, would be less important to the *Mapp* cases than in other areas of litigation. Harlan was Princeton educated, a Rhodes Scholar, and the grandson and namesake of Associate Justice John Marshall Harlan (1877-1911). Nominated by President Eisenhower to replace Justice Robert Jackson, Harlan was a solid force on the Court who eschewed judicial activism and was less than enthusiastic of the Warren revolution. Lastly, Potter Stewart, Eisenhower's fifth and last Supreme Court appointment was likeable and a solid and able jurist. He, like his father, spent most of his adult life in public service in Cincinnati and in Washington.

~~~

By the end of the 1955 term, it was clear that Warren's sway was toward the more liberal wing of the Court. The voices of Hugo Black and William Douglas resonated more so than the philosophy of judicial restraint of Felix Frankfurter. Cases concerning the rights of free speech by communist sympathizers and the thornier issue of racial inequality reveal a steady move to the left of center. Warren now saw the cases before him more as a jurist than a prosecutor. For Warren these were not issues of high intellectualism. They were issues of fairness, decency, and dignity. What emerges is a rights revolution based less on theory and more on pragmatism.

One catalyst for Warren's leadership in the "revolution" that was to come was appointed to the Court in 1956. William Brennan, President Eisenhower's replacement for Sherman Minton, would become Warren's most loyal and capable supporter. The first member of the Court to be born in the twentieth century, Brennan had been Felix Frankfurter's student at Harvard Law School. Any thoughts of allegiance were quickly dispelled. Brennan, charismatic, intellectually agile, and extremely hard working, became the lieutenant to Warren the general. The two would become judicial soulmates. Often they would discuss cases and judicial matters in long afternoon get-togethers in Brennan's chambers. The Chief Justice turned to Brennan for advice, and the able Brennan became a powerful ally and friend for Warren. Brennan and Warren, along with Black and Douglas, combined to overpower the judicial restraintist view of Frankfurter. The four formed a clear liberal coalition that only had to co-opt one additional justice to claim a majority. Often times that critical fifth justice was Tom Clark.

Any indecision or caution by Warren early in his infancy on the Court had vanished by 1956. In *Breithaupt v. Abram,*[30] Warren was emphatic that police misconduct would not be tolerated. Breithaupt, much like Rochin, had been involved in a traffic accident that called into question his sobriety behind the wheel. Whereas Rochin found his stomach pumped by police officers, Breithaupt was subjected to a withdrawal of his blood by attending physicians while unconscious. Some of the brethren made a distinction between the intrusions, arguing that pumping a suspect's stomach "shocked the conscience" of a civilized society while a blood sample obtained by a physician did not. Warren saw no such distinction. In a tersely worded dissent, he argued both violated due process. His position was clear: no matter that he had been a prosecutor and attorney general, police misconduct should and would be addressed by the Court. Warren's beliefs, in combination with his charismatic leadership, transformed the high bench from a generally conservative to more liberal institution.

Warren's leadership stemmed more from the nature of his personality than from sheer intellectual strength. His personal papers reveal a man of decency and kindness. His diplomacy was rarely fleeting. Even in dealing with the most

---

[30]   352 U.S. 432 (1957).

difficult of justices and their own personal feuds, Warren was dignified and firm in his resolution. For example, by late 1960 the relations between Justices Frankfurter and Douglas had so deteriorated that civility between them was rare. Mostly the two operated in a cold silence. Douglas finally could take no more of Frankfurter's professorial lectures and issued the following Memorandum to the Conference:

> The continuous violent outbursts against me in Conference by my Brother Frankfurter give me great concern. They do not bother me. But he's an ill man; and these violent outbursts create a fear in my heart that one of them may be his end. I do not consciously do anything to annoy him. But twenty-odd years have shown that I am a disturbing symbol in his life. His outbursts against me are increasing in intensity. In the interest of his health and long life I have reluctantly concluded to participate in no more conferences while he is on the Court. For the cert lists I will leave my vote. On argued cases I will leave a short summary of my views. W.O. D.[31]

Warren's response was to handle the two men in such a way that neither was offended, and both felt the Chief had understood and acted accordingly. Both expressed a sense of relief that the Chief empathized with their position. Warren viewed these personality clashes as part of the landscape of the high court. Such monumental brains and characters were bound to clash over the country's most contentious issues, but he seemed to take it all in stride. Warren's paper trail leaves the reader with the impression that he was a gentle giant. Not to be fooled, Warren got what he wanted; he just got it in such a way as to totally and unequivocally lead the Court.

Aiding in his success was his lieutenant William Brennan. Brennan quickly saw in Warren vision and wisdom. Brennan, too, was so very likeable and

---

[31]   Memorandum dated November 21, 1960, box 1234, William O. Douglas Papers, Library of Congress, Manuscript Room, Washington, D.C. To be fair, Douglas thought highly of Frankfurter's intellect. In his 1980 autobiography entitled *The Court Years: 1937-1975* (New York: Random House), Douglas compiled a list of the most outstanding justices with whom he served. He listed Frankfurter as one of the "All-American greats." See p. 42.

could make distinctions between a strident legal disagreement and professional harmony. His memoranda to his Brethren reflect a deference and respect that transcends any legal sparring: "Felix, did I correctly understand that if a state conviction resulted in this case...."[32] "Dear Tom, Of course you know I think this is just magnificent and wonderful."[33] Brennan circulated humorous as well as other weighty intellectual items to his colleagues. Clearly he adored Warren, giving him the title "Superchief." Brennan sent the Chief a cartoon, now yellow and faded, which depicts a man giving another a magic mirror. He asks it "Mirror, Mirror standing tall, who's the fairest one of all? Chief Justice Warren." Brennan attached a note that read, "Chief, Thems my sentiments!! I enthusiastically concur. I hope you and Nina will have a wonderful summer and a wonderful rest. Bill"[34]

Warren and Brennan's physical presence could not have been more different. Warren was a tall and solid stature, whereas Brennan was short, feisty, and reminded many of a leprechaun with his impish grin and twinkling eyes. But intellectually they were cut from the same cloth. Liberals from the same era, they were about the same age. The two settled into a routine of meeting late Thursday afternoons in Brennan's chambers to discuss the cases for Friday conference. Brennan provided Warren a sounding board and source of advice, and most importantly, friendship.

To look retrospectively at the Supreme Court in the 1960-61 term is to see nothing startling. By the start of the new decade in 1960, Americans seemed hopeful of the future. The front page of the *Cleveland Plain Dealer* on January 1, 1960, discussed little that would concern the court. On the heels of the decade of desegregation, the docket, while heavy, was the usual mix of cases.

---

32   Handwritten note from Justice Brennan to Justice Frankfurter, Box 62, William J. Brennan Papers, Library of Congress, Manuscript Room, Washington, D.C.

33   Note from Justice Brennan to Justice Tom Clark, May 1, 1961, Box 62, William J. Brennan Papers, Library of Congress, Manuscript Room, Washington, D.C.

34   Box 348 Earl Warren Papers, Library of Congress, Manuscript Room, Washington, D.C.

The number of docketed criminal cases was typical. The only unusual aspect of the Court's docket was its emphasis on communism. A rash of cases had made their way to the high bench concerning the liberties afforded those who disavowed democracy in favor of alternative forms of government. This issue consumed a good deal of the Court's docket as well as their intellectual energy. The precedential line of free speech cases, imprinted with the philosophical signature of Oliver Wendell Holmes, made headline news for the institution deciding such issues.

The *Mapp* case moved to the Court with little fanfare. The briefs by all parties indicated the free speech debate over possessing obscene material was the only real issue. Ohio's strict statute attempted to set the legal bar high for harboring pornography, making the mere possession of obscene material a felony. Merely possessing obscene material was a serious felony. This was no bombshell though. To the trained eye looking for landmark cases in the 1960 October term, *Dollree Mapp v. The State of Ohio* was an unlikely candidate.

CHAPTER EIGHT
The Oral Arguments

Walter Green's notice of appeal was filed June 15, 1960. Within a month, on July 14, 1960, the appeal was noted as received, and the Statement of Jurisdiction as well as a motion to dismiss or affirm was noted by the Court. The Supreme Court of the State of Ohio quickly responded, sending the exhibits to the Clerk of Courts on July19th and noting the acknowledgment of their receipt in Washington on July 25th.[1] For the remainder of the summer, the *Mapp* case lay dormant at the high bench. While Gertrude Mahon and Walter Green and his partner A. L. Kearns waited to hear if the Court would take the case, the rest of the country was engrossed in the presidential race of 1960. In mid-July the Democratic National Convention met in Los Angeles and nominated John F. Kennedy for president and Lyndon B. Johnson for vice president. A week and a half later, the Republicans met in Chicago and selected Richard M. Nixon and Henry Cabot Lodge for their choice as president and vice president respectively.

As summer turned to fall, the justices began to sift through their docket, noting probable jurisdiction, granting and denying certiorari, and beginning to hear cases in their courtroom. Just a week before, on September 26th, the youthful Senator John Kennedy took on the established and experienced Vice President Richard Nixon in the first-ever televised presidential debate. This was followed by a succession of debates on October 7th, 13th, and 21st. By the end of October the election was too close to call. The concerns of the American public were on the issues with which this new president was to grapple: the

---

[1]   Journal entry of the Supreme Court of the State of Ohio, Case No. 36091, microfilm Office of the Cuyahoga County Clerk of Court.

threat of communism, race relations, and civil rights. The election was decided on November 4th, with John Kennedy the winner by a hair. The selection of Kennedy in the closest election to date, would bring an alliance between the executive and judiciary that would tackle the ills of civil rights. Warren and Kennedy, both personally and professionally, respected and admired one another. Their combined efforts to grant Americans equality of opportunity and treatment would come to fruition a few years later. But for now, the Court's business was not center stage.

The October Term of 1960, or "OT1960," began on October the 3rd, the first Monday of October of that year. Several times a month the nine justices would vote to accept or deny cases appealed to them, docketing around 100 to 120 cases a term. Those cases accepted by the Court would then be scheduled for oral argument before the public in the Court's majestic courtroom. Afterward, each case would be assigned to one of the nine justices to represent the majority viewpoint. By internal rule and tradition, the most senior justice in the majority assigned the writing of the opinion that would reflect the prevailing viewpoint. The senior justice could either assign the opinion to himself or to another colleague in the majority. Strategy, as well as the equitable distribution of the workload, were factors. All told, the justices docketed 112 cases in the 1960 term, dividing the writing as follows:

Chief Justice Warren	14
Justice Black	16
Justice Frankfurter	15
Justice Douglas	16
Justice Clark	15
Justice Harlan	11

Justice Brennan   13
Justice Whittaker   12[2]

Each of the nine justices kept a docket book to record the legal path traveled by each case. Although similar in their notations of dates and outcomes, some of the justices made more candid remarks concerning the cases than their colleagues.[3]

Mapp's dormancy on the Court's docket ended on October 24th. The Court noted probable jurisdiction, with all of the justices voting in the affirmative except for Felix Frankfurter. Frankfurter voted to dismiss the case outright. Brennan noted on his docket sheet that Frankfurter's sentiments were "Possession under this statute with knowledge is a crime. This is substantive due process for me. It's not vague to me—it's clear."[4] Warren's notes reflect the same reasoning attributed to Frankfurter, only in a briefer form. "F.F.- substantive due process."[5] Despite the fact that eight of the nine justices agreed that the Court had jurisdiction, the grounds of review by the Court still varied. Again from the most complete docket books:

---

[2]   Box C76, File Assignment Lists, Tom Clark Papers, Tarlton Law Library, University of Texas at Austin.

[3]   Docket book of Justice Tom Clark, Box C76, Folder 201-400, Tom C. Clark Papers, Tarlton Law Library, University of Texas at Austin; Docket book of Earl Warren, Box 374, Folder Dockets OT1960, Library of Congress, Manuscript Room, Washington, D. C.; Docket book of William Brennan, Box 407, Library of Congress, Manuscript Room, Washington, D. C.; Docket book of William O. Douglas, Box 1233, Library of Congress, Manuscript Room, Washington, D. C

[4]   William J. Brennan's docket book on *Mapp v. Ohio*, Box 407, William Brennan Papers, Library of Congress Manuscript Room, Washington, D.C.

[5]   Earl Warren's docket book on *Mapp v. Ohio*. Box 374, Dockets OT 1960, Earl Warren Papers, Library of Congress, Manuscript Room, Washington, D.C.

WOD (Justice Douglas) - 1st Amend or overrides Wolf
TCC (Justice Clark) - Breadth of stat.
JMH (Justice Harlan) - Thought context of statute
WJB (Justice Brennan)- "___"
CEW (Chief Justice Warren) - Too Broad
PS (Justice Stewart) - Reexamining Alberts[6]

Warren's shorthand indicates the lack of consensus of the central issue at hand. Was this a First Amendment case or a Fourth Amendment one? Was the statute too vague because of its breadth and thus should be struck on these grounds alone? Clearly the Fourth Amendment had not crystalized as the core problem in the *Mapp* case. Brennan's notes confirm this array of opinions. For the Chief Justice he notes: "If put this one contraband, see no difference between this except cuts across first amendment rights. It's too broad a statute to accomplish its purpose and on that basis I'd reverse." Brennan notes no comment from Black in conference but indicates Douglas as stating, "I'd reverse on *Wolf* and on First Amendment." Harlan made clear that his problem with the statute was its overbearing nature: "Without any affect of determination, this is thought control. If wanted to put thoughts in a diary, this could reach it." Stewart noted, "If this stuff isn't covered by First and Fourteenth, I'd have trouble."[7] Without a consensus as to why, the Court took the case of *Mapp v. Ohio*, making it number 236 on the OT1960 docket.

The briefs in the case did little to crystalize the issue. Both Kearns and Mahon had focused on a variety of claims including the First Amendment, the Fourth Amendment, and Mapp's punishment. Concluded one of Warren's clerks: "The briefs of the parties in this case [*Mapp v. Ohio*] are among the worst I have seen all year. Happily, however, the amicus brief of the American Civil Liberties Union and Justice Taft's opinion in the court below tend to

---

6   Ibid. The full names next to the initials of each justice were added to assist the reader.

7   All comments taken from docket book of Justice William Brennan, Box 407, William J. Brennan Papers, Library of Congress, Manuscript Room, Washington, D. C.

bring the major issues into focus."[8] Since the written word was not compelling, the oral presentations in *Mapp* would prove an important forum for the justices to understand the case.

March 29, 1961, was the date set for the oral argument in *Mapp v. Ohio*. In open court, for one hour, the justices would focus on the events that had taken place so long ago on Milverton Road in Cleveland, Ohio. The Court personnel had changed, most notably with the addition of Justice Brennan. The country had changed too. And, most importantly, the law was about to change. The case, which was docketed with little notoriety, was about to begin its historic legacy in the U.S. Supreme Court.

"Oyez, oyez, oyez, All persons having business before the Honorable, the Supreme Court of the United States are admonished to draw near and give their attention for the Court is now sitting. God save the United States and God save this Honorable Court," so cried the Marshal on March 29th in the Court's beautiful marble courtroom. The climatic moment was now. The confluence of events was about to be distilled into sixty minutes of legal argument. Dollree Mapp's claim was about to be heard in the highest court in the land on Second Street in Washington, D.C. "Case number 236 Dollree Mapp versus the State of Ohio," called the Chief Justice on March 29, 1961, at ten o'clock in the morning. The nine justices had filed in behind the red velvet curtains that provided the backdrop to their curved oak bench. Facing the Court, the audience saw from left to right, Associate Justices Charles Whittaker, John Marshall Harlan, William O. Douglas, Hugo Black, and in the center chair, Chief Justice Earl Warren. Past Warren to the right was seated Associate Justices Felix Frankfurter, Tom Clark, William Brennan, and Potter Stewart. Called to the podium first was A. L. Kearns, the lawyer that Dolly had tried to reach by telephone on May 23, 1957, the day her house was searched.

---

8   Bench Memorandum for Chief Justice Warren, Box 210, Earl Warren Papers, Library of Congress, Manuscript Room, Washington, D. C.

Quickly and briefly, Kearns laid out the facts of the case, a bit more forcefully this time. His presentation began with a description of his client, Dollree Mapp. "She is a woman without any record whatsoever from the criminal point of view a decent, respectable American citizen."[9] The issue concerning the search warrant was raised quickly. Kearns stated that "the evidence discloses, at least two of the police officers who knew—one was Sergeant Delau—knew what he was there for, but made no effort to procure a search warrant. Neither one of them did. But they testified that a search warrant was procured by a Lieutenant White."[10] This however, wasn't exactly true. Delau had made an effort to obtain a search warrant. He had called Cooney who had tasked Lt. White to procure one. Delau, Haney, and Dever had waited outside Mapp's residence for the warrant to be delivered on-site before proceeding. Kearns did somewhat vindicate Delau by stating, "The evidence discloses that they were told that a search warrant had been procured."[11] Kearns called the document a "supposed search warrant" and when pressed, he said:

> There was no search warrant, Your Honor. Now the evidence discloses that no search warrant existed, although they claimed there was a search warrant. There is absolutely no evidence of any magistrate that had been asked for a search warrant; there was no record of a search warrant. We asked during the trial of the case that the search warrant be produced and it was not. The fact of the matter is that our own supreme court found that it was very questionable as to whether there was a search warrant in this case.[12]

> One of the justices inquires, "What was the piece of paper? Did that get identified?" Kearns: "We don't know what it was. She was not given an opportunity to read it."

Kearns even went so far as to explain that the police never produced the search warrant at trial by a clever feint.

---

9   Transcript of the oral arguments in *Mapp v. Ohio*, p. 1158.
10   Ibid., p. 1159.
11   Ibid., p. 1159.
12   Ibid., p. 1159-60.

I waited in the trial of the case for Lieutenant White, who was supposed to be the man
who procured the search warrant, to take the stand so that at least I could cross examine
him as to where, when and how he procured the search warrant and what the search
warrant contained. But the State was clever enough not to put him on the stand; and no
other police officer knew anything about it.[13]

It was pointed out that Kearns could have called White to the stand himself, but
a hostile witness could backfire. Kearns moved along to the obscenity issue,
distancing himself from his obvious frustration surrounding the circumstances
of the search. It is interesting, though, that despite the focus in the lower courts
on the issue of obscenity, the initial inquiry by the justices now concerned the
search of Mapp's home. Indeed, even Mapp's attorney chose to proceed with
the more tangential search and seizure problem rather than the obscenity
question.

Justice Frankfurter wanted even more specifics. "Are you asking us to
overrule the *Wolf* case in this Court? I notice it isn't even cited in your brief.
I just want to know what's before us, Mr. Kearns."[14] Kearns did not capitulate.
Moving to safer ground, he explained in detail the Ohio statute and the
consequences of the state supreme court ruling in terms of the First
Amendment. This raised the issue of whether or not the statute was
constitutional. Kearns interjected that also before the Court was "the search and
seizure proposition in this case." Frankfurter asked again, "Well, that means
you're asking us to overrule *Wolf against Colorado*." Kearns reply is
significant for the later reach of the Court. "No. I don't believe we are. All that
we're asking is that we have this *Lindway* that I'm setting forth in our brief that
is controlling the entire State of Ohio."[15] (Recall that *Lindway* established the
idea that even illegally seized evidence is admissible.) Again, Kearns

---

[13]   Ibid., p. 1160.

[14]   Ibid., p. 1164.

[15]   Ibid., pp. 165-66.

exchanged clarifying comments with the justices concerning what relief he was seeking from the court.

> Court: "Is the question that there was an unlawful search, is that in controversy in this case?"
> Kearns: "No, it isn't."
> Court: "All right."
> Kearns: "There was an unlawful search."[16]

Kearns goes on to criticize *Lindway* for disregarding the method of obtaining evidence, while concentrating only on the quality and probative value of the evidence. He lamented the state statute but never argued the broader issue of *Wolf v. Colorado*, the Supreme Court precedent for the case at hand. The Court did address the obscenity question but only after beginning with the Fourth Amendment question. Given the grounds for appeal, this lengthy probing exchange about the Fourth Amendment's reach was surprising. Kearns was over half way through his oral argument and the obscenity issue had not even been addressed.

The location of the obscene items was a concern to several justices since the Ohio statute of "mere possession" begged the question of what fact determined possession. Without reference to specific locale, Kearns explained, possession was broadly interpreted. Some of the justices found it hard to believe that the lower court had not teased out the facts surrounding the obscenity statute as it applied to the specific facts here. If the material was found in the basement rather than her bedroom would that make a difference? Was there any dispute in the record that the material in question had indeed been found to be obscene? The complaint seemed generalized, and quickly several justices asked for clarification. The obscenity question and the search that produced the material in question were becoming more and more

---

[16]   Ibid., pp. 1167-69.

intertwined. Finally the Court asked Kearns to make the connection, or lack of one, clear.

"May I trouble you to tell us what you deem to be the questions that are open before this Court?" Kearns was asked. As he answered by reciting portions of 2905.34 concerning the possession of obscene material, he was interrupted and asked, "Well, that's the only question we've got here, as to whether the statute's constitutional or not constitutional, isn't it?" Kearns's reply broadened *Mapp*'s concern beyond the obscenity questions as first proposed.

> Kearns: "Two questions, as we see it. Very respectfully submitted is the question of: Is the statute constitutional under which she was convicted? And the search and seizure proposition in this case."[17]

Frankfurter pressed further. "Well, that means you're asking us to overrule *Wolf against Colorado*."

Feeling the wrath that might follow if he was to ask for something here that he had not addressed in his written brief, Kearns replied "No." He claimed that the concern was *Lindway*. Again he was led to a legal position that was indefensible, widening his claim in orals that he had not supported with written documentation.

> The court: "And that (*Lindway*) holds that, although evidence is illegally procured, it is admissible, right?"
> Kearns: "That's right."
> The court: "And that's the familiar doctrine in so many states in this Union, and which we dealt with in the *Wolf* case. You don't even refer to it in your brief."

Kearns had to admit that, true, he had not made much of *Wolf* in his brief, but perhaps the state had addressed it. He did assert, "But the fact of the matter

---

17   Ibid., pp. 1164-66.

is that we are, as citizens of Ohio, deprived of our constitutional rights against unlawful search and seizure."[18]

The dance between the attorney and justices continued, and Kearns held on as best he could. "Did you raise the question of no search warrant in the trial court?" Kearns replied in the affirmative, noting that he had taken the additional step of filing a motion to suppress that was overruled. Kearns went on to point out that the suppression ruling was due to *Lindway*, which was controlling in Ohio state courts.

As Kearns's oral presentation was nearing the end, he turned to the length of sentence that Mapp received. He argued that the indeterminate nature of one to seven years was cruel and unusual. It was clear by the Court's response that the Eighth Amendment provision referred more to the type of punishment than to the length of it. Kearns then quickly gave the remainder of his time to Bernard Berkman of the Ohio Civil Liberties Union.

Kearns's presentation was not clear and convincing, but it was not a disaster for his client either. Most of the clarity of his argument was teased out by the justices themselves, rather than the insights brought to the podium by Kearns. He appeared frustrated and unsure of what the core of his argument should be. He eventually conceded that the search component was part of his defense, yet surprisingly, he did not cite *Wolf* or argue it. Surely he would have anticipated that the search question would be fully explored, but perhaps not. The focus of Mapp's attorney was more on the inequities stemming from the obscenity statute rather than the search.

The first sentence out of the mouth of Bernard Berkman seized the opportunity afforded Kearns.

I would like to say that the American Civil Liberties Union and its Ohio affiliate, the Ohio Civil Liberties Union, is very clear, in response to the question which was directed to counsel for the appellant, that we are asking this Court to reconsider *Wolf versus Colorado* and to find that evidence which is unlawfully and illegally obtained

---

[18]   Ibid., pp. 1166.

should not be permitted into a state proceeding, and that its production is a violation
of the Federal Constitution, the Fourth Amendment and the Fourteenth Amendment.
We have no hesitancy about asking the Court to reconsider it because we think that it
is a necessary part of due process.[19]

"Are you asking us to re-examine *Wolf*, or are you relying on *Rochin*
against California?" asked the Court. Without hesitation Berkman replied, "We
are asking the Court to re-examine *Wolf*. Our interest is not necessarily the
same as that of the defendant who was convicted in this case, and our claim is
more broad than that."[20] *Mapp* was a vehicle for civil libertarians looking to
incorporate more of the Bill of Rights and to complete the process that *Wolf*
had started. Not forgetting that his participation in the case was due to other
interests, Berkman informed the Court that his primary purpose was to urge the
justices to declare the Ohio obscenity statute unconstitutional. Without a doubt,
a revisitation of *Wolf* was primary to Berkman's agenda.

After attacking the search violation, Berkman moved on to the obscenity
statute. He conceded that "by any definition which this Court would choose to
apply, the material was obscene, and for our purposes we are assuming that to
be the fact." He goes on to say that: "We deplore the appellant's bad taste in the
selection of her literature. [But] as we see it, the central issue in considering the
validity of this statute is this: Is this an area in which the individual has the
right to be let alone, to be free of governmental restraint?" This provoked the
pointed question, "Are you asking us to reconsider *Roth*?"

Berkman again without hesitation replied, "We are asking you to reconsider
Roth, in addition to the other." Berkman was abruptly stopped with
Frankfurter's quip, "You're asking for a lot today."[21] Indeed he was. Berkman
asked for far more than *Mapp*'s attorney, asking for changes in the law beyond
the relief of one Dollree Mapp. Berkman stepped back a bit when he said, "We

---

[19]   Ibid., p. 1170.
[20]   Ibid., p. 1170.
[21]   Ibid., p. 1174.

do not feel it necessary to consider whether the Fourth Amendment is incorporated bodily into the Fourteenth Amendment. We think that certainly the right of privacy is a basic concept of freedom which appears here."[22] At this point, perhaps his goal was to inform the justices of the problem and let them arrive at the solution they saw fit. Both the First and Fourth Amendment violations were substantial. *Wolf*, which allowed states to devise their own remedy for Fourth violations, was penned by Berkman's most intense questioner, Justice Frankfurter. He had made his point. Berkman quickly wrapped up his comments.

The Chief Justice then called Gertrude Mahon to the podium. Arguing on behalf of the state of Ohio, Mahon got off to a poor start. She began by revealing that one of the state's exhibits had disappeared, indicating that only the cover and not the contents of one of the obscene books was returned to the Court of Common Pleas. All had conceded that the missing material was obscene, but Mahon's primary concern was that she had not introduced the cover as the exhibit but the book itself. Moving quickly to the statutory question, the question of guilt by merely possessing obscene material, she was asked, tongue in cheek, " Has the Clerk been indicted?"[23] After the laughter subsided, Mahon found herself delineating the finer points of the word possession.

Justice Brennan asked her if it is unlawful to possess obscene material, couldn't the clerk of the Court, the Court and even the prosecution be in violation of the Ohio statute? She replied "No," since the statute referred to unlawful possession such as possession with the intent to circulate. Brennan found her reasoning circular. "Your supreme court in this very case has construed this as meaning that if you have possession, naked possession, with knowledge that it's obscene, you're guilty of a crime under the statute."

---

[22]   Ibid., p. 1175.

[23]   Ibid., p. 1176.

Mahon: "That is right. But inherent in the element of possession is the opportunity for circulation, wouldn't you say, Mr. Justice Brennan?"

Brennan retorted: "It is not what I'm saying; it's what your supreme court is saying."[24]

Still unconvinced about what the statute meant by punishing for possession, Mahon was asked about book collectors by one of the justices.

On a bookshelf, merely as part of his library, he's a bibliophile and he collects first editions, not for the contents, but because it's a first edition. And any book on his shelves, on my shelves which I know to be obscene in content, but a matter of great indifference to me because I'm interested in the fact that it was published in 1527, that makes me a violator of the statute? Is that correct?

Mrs. Mahon: "I would say so, Your Honor; any collector of obscenity would be...."

The courtroom broke out in laughter at the absurdity of her conclusion.

She finished her thought. "...would be violating this statute."

Frankfurter noted, "Well, Uncle Sam has one of the biggest collections (referring to the Library of Congress), and I can tell you now where it is, but it's outside of your jurisdiction."

The audience in the courtroom laughed again. The extremities of such a position weakened her core argument. She knew it, as did everyone else. If she stuck to her original argument, possession with regard to circulation, such a rationale could hardly be applied to a book collector or a library's holdings. Shortly thereafter, Mahon conceded some weaknesses of the Ohio statute that would prosecute Mapp for involuntarily possessing obscene material that belonged to someone else. She was grilled about interpreting the statute in such a way that Mapp, who was merely providing storage for someone else's items that were obscene, was just as guilty as the owner of the items. Mahon conceded the problem in prosecuting individuals who have possession, whether it is primary possession, temporary possession, or true control over the items:

---

24   Ibid., p. 1178.

the statute made no distinctions. Her defense of the state's position became more timid. It also became more problematic.

At one point Mahon equated possession of narcotics and possession of obscene literature as constitutionally one and the same. She was immediately met with the pointed question posed by one of the justices, "Really, your constitutional argument, if I understand it correctly, from *Roth*, is that *Roth* says obscene literature is not protected, and therefore it's just like contraband, and therefore the State can do anything they want with it." Gertrude Mahon replied, "It is within the police power, yes. Yes, that is our position."[25] Her argument asserted the right of states to govern on behalf of their citizens' health, safety, welfare, and morality. This was the quintessential mission of state government as she saw it.

The Court allowed her to ramble a bit, moving from the obscenity question and back again to the search and seizure question. It was clear she was not in control of the orals and was unsure of where a firmer ground lay. For example, she flustered a bit with her position on the quality of the search and the exclusion of the evidence. "I have never been able to reconcile—that is, not reconcile; but it seems to me." Then she argued for maintaining the position the Court held in *Wolf v. Colorado*.

> (T)hat the provision in the Constitution against an unreasonable search and seizure and the competency of evidence establishing the commission of a crime are not directly related in this respect: that the absence of a search warrant can be no defense to a crime. If the evidence establishes a crime, what defense is there in the absence of a search warrant? It's a collateral matter. It provides for a civil suit for trespass if that constitutional right is violated. Police officers are amenable to—as held in the *Lindway* case, to an action for such trespass.

Mahon had returned to the common law remedy referred to as early as *Boyd v. United States* in 1886. "And so, in the Ohio constitution and under the Ohio

---

[25] Ibid, p. 1184.

laws, the fact that there was a search warrant would not make the evidence any the more competent or the fact that there was no search warrant would not make it any the less competent. It has no bearing whatsoever on the evidence itself." Her argument concerning possession, the central core of the case, was weak and was repeatedly met with the ire of some of the justices and even provoked laughter. However, her position on the search and seizure of Dollree Mapp was doctrinally solid. She was asking the Court to maintain the status quo. Allow the states, again on the basis of state police powers, to govern the remedy for search and seizure violations. She was not asking, as Berkman had, for a lot. She was not asking for the law to be changed. She only asserted the right of the state, in both the First and Fourth Amendment, on police powers grounds, to safeguard the welfare of their citizens. Her position on the Fourth Amendment had become her stronger argument.

Again the justices forced her to return to her more difficult position on obscenity. She assisted them by her comments regarding privacy.

> Well, under your *Roth* case you held that the Constitution doesn't protect obscenity in any respect. The right to read, and they said the right of privacy, and that's getting back to having books in your private library. If under the Roth case the Constitution doesn't protect the collection of obscenity, then I say that you can't have them in your private library either.

Frankfurter pounced on her. "Have you made an examination of the library of the State University of Ohio or Western Reserve or Wooster, or scores, you've got scores of colleges, I suppose, that are esteemed. I haven't been told, but my guess, is, probably more than any other State in the Union. Would the various prosecutors, certainly, they've got possession of the books in their library, wouldn't you think so, in any view of possession?"

Mahon replied that she would not agree that any of the libraries that Justice Frankfurter had mentioned would contain any type of book as introduced in this case. Frankfurter found her position indefensible. He claimed that as institutions of learning, of course they would possess material that would be condemned. "Pornography itself is a subject for learning, a very important one."[26]

But Mahon would not surrender so easily. "I would find it difficult to believe, without even examining those university libraries, that those libraries would contain what has been passed upon by a jury in this case as obscene material. And if that were so, if any one of those libraries contained the obscene books and pictures that are to be found as exhibits in this case, then somebody should be arrested."[27] An incredible argument, one that was practically indefensible.

"Maybe it would be wiser not to discuss the university libraries much further, for the benefit of the university libraries," one of the justices commented. Seeing herself off the hook, she replied, "That is true." "Well, of course, I'm trying to stick to the past in this case, Your Honor. I'm not covering the whole field of...." She never finishes the sentence with "pornography." Again the courtroom erupted in laughter. "But we're examining a statute of general application," reminded one of the justices.[28]

Herein lay the fundamental problem of defending the Ohio statute. One could not merely possess materials of questionable content because the law did not determine how the individual obtained it, whether they were in control of it, or what their intent was. Possession was the only thing that mattered. The oral arguments made clear that this interpretation by Ohio would surely find disfavor. Its breadth, indeed its overbreadth, would be grounds for striking the statute. Mahon herself noted that the reach of the law was problematic even for her, the state's attorney. One justice noted: "You're not in a very good position to disagree with the interpretation that your supreme court puts on your Act, are

---

26 Ibid, p. 1187.
27 Ibid, p. 1187.
28 Ibid, p. 1187.

you?" Mahon replied solemnly, "No." "Not in this Court, anyway." noted the justice.[29]

Gertrude Mahon concluded her argument by asking the Court to do nothing more than stay the course.

> Your Honors, we believe, the State of Ohio, that we have a right to rely on your decision in the *Wolf* case and on your decision in the *Roth* case, if there is anything to the doctrine of stare decisis;[30] and that we also, the trial court had a right to rely on the *Lindway* decision in handling this matter in the trial court, because the *Lindway* decision is in line with your decision in the *Wolf* case.[31]

In the final moments of Mahon's orals, the Court returned to the nagging question of the search warrant in the Mapp case. "Is the search warrant in existence?" asked one of the justices. Mahon replied that "Insofar as the record is concerned, it doesn't show any." Mahon quickly recapped the arguments surrounding the securing of a search warrant. She noted that Delau and Haney had nothing to do with the actual search warrant request. "When the defendant requested, told them (Delau and Haney) to get one, the officers said they waited and that Lieutenant White came out there. They thought he had a search warrant. Now, that's what the record shows."[32] The comment by Mahon, that they, meaning the two officers who conducted the search, thought he (White) had a search warrant, would be essential to the future of the exclusionary rule. Without realizing it, Mahon had laid the groundwork for the good faith exception. This would be the salvation that the Cleveland police would relish,

---

[29]   Ibid, p. 1190.

[30]   The Latin term *stare decisis* translates "let the decision stand." The interpretation of *stare decisis* is that the current decision maker will abide by the previous decisions, in other words, uphold precedence.

[31]   Transcript of Oral Arguments in *Mapp v. Ohio*, p. 1195.

[32]   Ibid., p. 1197; emphasis added.

but it would not come until 1984.[33] Chief Justice Warren then thanked Gertrude Mahon, her presentation complete.

The oral arguments in the case of *Dollree Mapp v. The State of Ohio* were over. Both Kearns and Mahon had found the search question more debatable than the obscenity question. It seemed clear that the Ohio law would fall due to its vagueness. Neither lawyer made a strong case for its use. The search and seizure question was much more unclear. Should *Wolf* prevail? Was *Lindway* in keeping with the *Wolf* doctrine? By the afternoon of this March day, those questions seemed paramount to the outcome of *Mapp v. Ohio*, more so than the obscenity question.

---

[33] The good-faith exception to the exclusionary rule was established in the companion cases *U.S. v. Leon*, 468 U.S. 897 and *Massachusetts v. Sheppard*, 468 U.S. 981 (1984).

CHAPTER NINE
Opinion Writing

Just two days later, March 31, 1961, the nine Justices met in their regular Friday conference to discuss the cases they had heard in oral arguments that week and to assign the writing of the majority opinions in each of them. When docket number 236 was presented, "The discussion continued to be devoted almost entirely to the constitutionality of the Ohio obscenity statute."[1] It was not difficult for the Brethren to come to an agreement on the state law. Justice Harlan's docket book reflects this consensus.[2] While there was widespread agreement on the state obscenity statute, there was considerable debate about the search and seizure question and the fate of *Wolf v. Colorado*. Justice Douglas indicated to the others that although there was no majority willing to rule on Fourth Amendment grounds, he found the facts in *Mapp* violated both the First and Fourteenth Amendments. Chief Justice Warren and Justice Brennan were in agreement. Still the tie that bound the majority coalition hinged on the First Amendment. Clark too had indicated his interest in seeing *Wolf* overturned (remember his earlier comments regarding the Fourth Amendment in *Irvine v. California*). However, there was no consensus. The only majority that existed in *Mapp v. Ohio* at the first conference was on the

---

[1]   Bernard Schwartz, *Super Chief: Earl Warren and His Supreme Court* (New York: New York University Press, 1983), p. 392.

[2]   Found in Box 356, Earl Warren Papers, Library of Congress, Manuscript Room, Washington, D.C. In fact, the docket books of each of the justices reflect this similar understanding of the issues presented in the *Mapp* case. Each of the docket books were consulted with the exception of Justice Potter Stewart's. Stewart's Supreme Court papers are located at Yale University but are closed to research.

fate of the Ohio obscenity law. Clark was selected to write the majority opinion.

Clark swiftly realized the opportunity *Mapp* provided. "On the elevator after leaving the conference room, the Texan turned to Black and Brennan and asked, "Wouldn't this be a good case to apply the exclusionary rule and do what *Wolf* didn't do?"[3] The focus of Bernard Berkman's brief resonated. If indeed the search of Mapp's home was illegal, should the evidence be excluded? Was this the opportunity to change *Wolf*? Was this the case that would incorporate the remedy that corresponded with *Wolf's* Fourth Amendment right? Clark was intrigued enough to consider the possibility. No doubt he found support in Brennan, but the author of *Wolf*, Frankfurter, was horrified. On the question of search and seizure Clark could rely on Warren, Brennan, and Douglas. He was one vote shy of a majority opinion that would adjudicate *Mapp* as a Fourth Amendment case. Still, the two-prong approach to Fourth Amendment violations could and would be revisited by the Court. Despite the lack of oral arguments on the matter, or briefs that fully explored the implications for the Fourth Amendment, *Mapp v. Ohio* was in the process of being transformed from a First Amendment case to a Fourth Amendment one.

Clark's drafting of *Mapp* was thorough. He asked his clerks[4] to write a memorandum on writs of assistance. The document grew to nine pages in length, which Clark read and heavily edited. It is clear he understood the history of the Fourth Amendment passage and its consequences both in common law and practice. In addition, he had his clerks list and briefly note every Supreme Court case decided on Fourth Amendment grounds. The memorandum noted each case and often quoted or summarized the decision. In

---

[3]   Bernard Schwartz, *Super Chief*, p. 393.
[4]   Carl Estes III, who is referred to in Clark's papers as CLE, and Malachy Mahon, who is referred to as MTM.

the margins next to *United States v. Jeffers*[5] a clerk noted "This language hurts us because it says [the] exclusionary rule is court made and implies Congress can change it and particularly because Clark, J. said it."[6] Other cases provided some utility to Clark. "Excellent language in support of idea that Weeks' exclusionary rule is constitutional mandate."[7] It was obvious in the early drafting of the *Mapp* opinion that Clark and his clerks realized the significance of their decision. Critics would argue that the remedy was not rooted in the Constitution but merely a judicial creation. Lacking constitutional status, the exclusionary rule was subject to the creativity of lawmakers who could devise whatever remedy for Fourth violations that they saw fit. In other words, the choices of *Wolf* were still available. Exclusion, it could be argued, was not a mandated remedy for Fourth Amendment violations but merely the Court's preference. If Clark were to use *Mapp* as the vehicle to overturn Wolf, *stare decisis* was not always favorable.

His caution in crafting the *Mapp* decision is admirable. Indeed Clark's concern for the constitutional status of the exclusionary rule drove his clerks to delve into the composition of the court that decided *Weeks v. United States*, (1914).

> Can we show that the first hint that *Weeks'* exclusion rule was a rule of evidence and not of constitutional mandate came about after the membership of the Weeks court was completely gone? And before that complete turnover what ever references there were to the *Weeks'* rule were cast in terms, explicit or ambiguous, of a constitutional rule?[8]

---

[5]   342 U.S. 48 (1951).

[6]   Box A210, Folder 7, Tom Clark Papers, Tarlton Law Library, University of Texas at Austin, Austin, Texas.

[7]   In reference to *Olmstead v. United States*, 277 U.S. 438 (1928). Box A210, Folder 7, Tom Clark Papers, Tarlton Law Library, University of Texas at Austin, Austin, Texas.

[8]   See memo, Box A115, Folder 7, Tom Clark Papers, Tarlton Law Library, The University of Texas Law Library, Austin, Texas.

The memo traces the composition of the *Weeks* court (1913-14) and when each of the justices left the court. Clark was trying to document that the *Weeks* court saw the exclusionary rule as deriving from the Constitution. Only after the *Weeks* justices left the Court were there references to the nonconstitutional status of the rule of exclusion. This very debate would be raised again shortly after the *Mapp* decision and would continue until the Court's decision in *United States v. Calandra*,[9] *United States v. Janis*,[10] and *Stone v. Powell*.[11]

Clark circulated his first draft on April 28, 1961. Attached to the draft sent to Hugo Black was the following note. "Hugo—At your convenience I would appreciate your criticisms. This is the first draft and will need some "polishing." On the reference to Chicago and N.Y. we have some statistics that refute the assumption that private remedy (damages, prosecution of the officers, etc) afford any relief. Thanks—TCC."[12] Clark argued in this first draft that "Of the 37 states passing on the Weeks exclusionary rule since the Wolf decision, 21 have either adopted or adhered to the rule. While in 1949 almost two thirds of the states were opposed to the rule, now 57% of those passing upon it approve. Thus, while 66% admitted the evidence in 1949, only 48% presently adhere to that rule."[13] Clark made the parallel to *Irvine*, noting that most jurisdictions would find the opposite result today. Armed with statistics and evidence of the changing times, Clark argued that the exclusionary rule was the logical result of such trends. Central to his argument was the idea that more and more states were using the exclusionary rule as the appropriate remedy for Fourth Amendment violations.

Clark pointed out the inconsistency of a federal exclusionary rule but no corresponding state remedy. Under the federal system, some arrests were undoubtedly lost. Quoting Cardozo, Clark conceded that at times the "criminal

---

[9]   414 U.S. 338 (1974).

[10]   428 U.S. 433 (1976).

[11]   428 U.S. 465 (1976).

[12]   Box 349, Hugo Black Papers, Library of Congress, Manuscript Room, Washington, D.C.

[13]   Draft by Tom Clark, Majority opinion in *Mapp v. Ohio*, p. 3.

is to go free because the constable has blundered." But "The Amendment's protection [can be] made effective for everyone only by upholding it when invoked by the worst of men."[14] Clark took the position that society as a whole benefits despite the windfall that comes to the few. His language indicated his distaste for only a federal exclusionary rule. He argued that Elkins "disemboweled" the silver platter doctrine and the idea that states were immune from a uniform remedy.

For Clark, judicial integrity and integrity of government as a whole were paramount.

> To say that a government should be able to use unconstitutionally seized evidence because there is no fundamental prohibition against its use of evidence seized unlawfully by private persons, is to ignore the experience of ages. What can destroy a government more quickly than its failure to observe its own laws, or worse, its disregard of the charter of its own existence?[15]

After all, if the criminal goes free, it is the law that makes him free. The logic of Clark's sweeping argument is hard to refute. This rationale of the exclusionary rule, to preserve judicial integrity, would remain a central component of the *Mapp* argument. States had to provide the same guarantee as the federal government. Allowing any judicial system to profit from illegality undermined the very existence of the judicial system. Handwritten in the margins is "However much in a particular case insistent upon such rules may appear as a technicality that is sure to be to the benefit of a guilty person, the history of criminal law proves that tolerance of shortcut methods in law enforcement impairs its enduring effectiveness."[16]

---

14   Clark is quoting here the dissenting opinion in *Abel v. United States*, 362 U.S. 217, 248. He would later remove this particular language from the opinion but not the idea.

15   Draft by Tom Clark, majority opinion in *Mapp v. Ohio*, p. 10.

16   Quoting from *Miller v. United States*, 357 U.S. 301, 313 (1958) in Clark's draft of the majority opinion in *Mapp v. Ohio*, Folder 1, Tom Clark Papers, Tarlton Law Library, University of Texas at Austin, Austin, Texas.

The core of Clark's opinion would not be altered much by his colleagues, but Clark was wise in attempting to build consensus for his draft. His request to Black was genuine. Indeed Clark's private papers reveal correspondence with Black and Douglas *even before* Clark released his first draft on April 28th. On April 25th Clark sent a note to Black: "Dear Hugo: I hope this is better. I have re-arranged and inserted new material. Thanks for the suggestions. TCC."[17] Clark's early drafts indicate substantial revisions and additions due to Black's input. A note of April 29, 1961: "Dear Tom: That is a mighty fine opinion you have written in No. 236 – *Mapp v. Ohio*. Please join me in it. William O. Douglas."[18] Other justices too felt compelled to express their views. By early May, Clark had heard from Brennan saying that he would join. "May 1, 1961 RE: No. 236 - *Mapp v. Ohio* Dear Tom: Of course you know I think this is just magnificent and wonderful. I have not joined anything since I came with greater pleasure. Sincerely, Bill"[19] The Chief Justice joined as well. In a letter dated May 2nd the Chief writes simply, "Dear Tom: RE: NO. 236 - *Mapp v. Ohio* I agree. E.W."[20]

However, both Potter Stewart and John Marshall Harlan indicated their reservations of Clark's early draft. Stewart responded on May 1st that "As I am sure you anticipated, your proposed opinion in this case came as quite a surprise." Stewart then laid out his concerns succinctly and forcefully. His writings indicate strong reservations. It would seem that Stewart was a clear dissent.

---

[17]   Box A115, Folder 6, Tom Clark Papers, Tarlton Law Library, The University of Texas at Austin, Austin, Texas.

[18]   Box A115, Folder 6, Tom Clark Papers, Tarlton Law Library, The University of Texas at Austin, Austin, Texas.

[19]   Box A115, Folder 6, Tom Clark Papers, Tarlton Law Library, The University of Texas at Austin, Austin, Texas.

[20]   Box 474, Earl Warren Papers, Library of Congress Manuscript Room, Washington, D.C.

In all honesty, I seriously question the wisdom of using this case as a vehicle to overrule an important doctrine so recently established and so consistently adhered to. I point out only that the idea of overruling *Wolf* was urged in the brief and oral arguments only by amicus curiae and was not even discussed at the Conference, where we all agreed, as I recollect it, that the judgment should be reversed on First Amendment grounds. If *Wolf* is to be reconsidered I myself would much prefer to do so only in a case that required it, and only after argument of the case by competent counsel and a full Conference discussion. Sincerely yours, P.S.[21]

Stewart's concerns would undermine, albeit only temporarily. The First Amendment case turned Fourth Amendment case would long be remembered for its search and seizure violation and little else. Stewart was unwilling to use *Mapp* as the vehicle for change that Clark so eagerly asserted on the Court's back elevator. True to his early views, Stewart would remain consistent in adjudicating *Mapp v. Ohio* as it had been presented originally to the Court: as a First Amendment obscenity case. Clark's notations in the margins of Stewart's memorandum indicate that he understood Stewart's position clearly.

Harlan's response to Clark's first draft was more acerbic. His three and a half pages ended with the by-then obvious conclusion, "Perhaps you will have gathered from the foregoing that I would not be about to join you in your present opinion!" He, like Stewart, believed a consensus was reached on the constitutionality of the Ohio statute and that *Mapp* was an unwise vehicle to alter the ruling in *Wolf*. However, it is Harlan's claims concerning *Wolf*, *Weeks*, and *Mapp* which force Clark to sharpen his opinion. Harlan methodically outlines why "your proposed overruling of *Wolf* is, both unnecessary and inadvisable." At the heart of the claim is the constitutionality of the exclusionary rule. "I am not yet ready to hold (and I do not think the cases compel us to hold) that the Weeks rule is constitutionally based, that is, that Congress could not pass a statute rendering illegally seized, though relevant, evidence admissible in a federal criminal trial." He continued, "What is it, may

---

[21]   Box A115, Folder 6, Tom Clark Papers, Tarlton Law Library, The University of Texas at Austin, Austin, Texas.

I ask, that should lead us at this juncture to say in effect that a State which has no "exclusionary" experience has been unfortunate is henceforth constitutionally forbidden to revert to a 'non-exclusionary' policy?"[22] In other words, Harlan viewed the exclusionary rule as non-constitutionally based. Therefore it allowed legislative bodies to come to a decision about the admissibility of evidence in their state courts. It was up to legislatures to decide, as the Court had decreed in *Wolf v. Colorado*. As long as the Fourth Amendment right was not violated, the remedy was left to the state legislative body. For Harlan, the precedent of *Wolf v. Colorado* was a sound one.

At the heart of Harlan's memorandum was the thorny problem of the exclusionary rule's origin. If it was judicially created, as some had argued in *Wolf v. Colorado*, then its constitutional status was less secure than rules that emanated from the text of the Constitution itself. This quibble over the origin of the exclusionary rule was not trivial. Indeed the rule's future would hinge on the debate of its origin. Some of the jurists believed that the legality of a search could be separated from criminal proceedings. The result of a Fourth Amendment violation was a separate question, one subject to the decision of a judge separate from the trial outcome. However, other Court members felt the exclusionary rule required judges to protect constitutional violations, Fourth Amendment violations, and that this was integral to what the framers of the Constitution had in mind. Harlan felt that the exclusionary rule was not embedded in the Constitution as Clark argued in his draft. *Wolf* made that clear and the facts of *Mapp* did little to change the status quo.

Harlan was also concerned by the suggestion that *Weeks* and *Wolf* lent support to the application of the exclusionary rule to the states through the Fourteenth Amendment. The incorporation debate, that the Bill of Rights must or must not be applied to the states through the addition of the Fourteenth Amendment, was an unnecessary addition to the increasing controversy of the

---

[22] Memorandum of Justice John Marshall Harlan, Box A115, Folder 6, Tom Clark Papers, Tarlton Law Library, The University of Texas at Austin, Austin, Texas.

rule of exclusion. Harlan even added in a handwritten postscript, "If you don't mind my saying so, your opinion comes perilously close to accepting 'incorporation' for the Fourth A., and will doubtless encourage the 'incorporation' enthusiasts."[23]

Harlan saw little in Clark's opinion that he could agree with. For Harlan, *Mapp v. Ohio* did not present the Court with an opportunity to address these serious and weighty constitutional issues. "The upshot of all this is that I earnestly ask you to reconsider the advisability of facing the Court, in a case which otherwise should find a ready and non-controversial solution, with the controversial issues that your proposed opinion tenders."[24] And Clark had no choice but to consider the concerns Harlan had forcefully set forth in his memorandum. Clark had yet to hear from Frankfurter, the author of *Wolf*. No doubt Frankfurter would agree with Harlan's assessment of the reach of Clark's opinion.

Justice Clark began working on a response to Harlan almost immediately. By May 3rd he had drafted a memo aimed more at defending his position than attempting to convert Harlan. Like any good lawyer or politician, Clark began by pointing out to Harlan their areas of agreement.

> You are quite right with regard to the mere possession of obscene material as a possible First Amendment violation, but, of course, as was pointed out in the Conference, it clearly raises the *Wolf* question to which was made direct reference in the opinion of the Ohio Supreme Court.[25]

Clark even noted that during conference, three justices indicated that the Fourth Amendment problem was an "alternative ground for reversal." While Clark admitted that all controversial cases were grounds for disagreement, "I have a court and therefore my theory has support." Clark again reiterated the growing

---

23   Ibid.
24   Ibid.
25   Ibid.

popularity of the exclusionary rule in state law and his belief, along with those of others, that *Weeks* is a constitutionally based rule.

> I believe our opinions support this—even *Wolf* says it is a constitutional rule formulated by 'judicial implication.' Applying the exclusionary rule to the states in *Mapp*, quite frankly I believe achieves a necessary measure of symmetry in our constitutional doctrine on both federal and state exercise of those powers incident to their enforcement of criminal law."[26]

Clark stated firmly that if the incorporationists received a windfall in *Mapp* "then *Wolf* brought it on." Clark ended his response to Harlan in a professional manner. "I hope that you will restudy the opinion, John, and find logic and reason in it. If you have any suggestions I shall welcome them. Yours, TCC."[27]

In addition to responding to Justice Harlan, on May 4th Clark recirculated his draft, this time including a description of the facts of the case. His tone reflected his feelings that the search of Dollree Mapp's home was highly irregular. For example he added in the margins, "The entire floor was ransacked as was the basement." His factual statement about the search of Mapp's home, the lack of evidence that a search warrant existed, and the egregiously high level of intrusion expanded to several pages. Eventually such inflammatory language was tempered into a more concise statement, yet Clark's sense of fairness was clearly tweaked. Without a doubt, he felt that the police violated Mapp's rights and his factual statement was a strong endorsement of that idea. The remainder of Clark's opinion essentially remained the same. By now Clark's draft included the language that Harlan and Stewart would act differently (meaning not agree with Clark's draft). He also noted that "Mr. Justice Frankfurter will in due course file a separate opinion."

---

26 Memorandum of Justice Clark to Justice Harlan, Box A115 Folder 6, Tom Clark Papers, Tarlton Law Library, The University of Texas at Austin, Austin, Texas.

27 Ibid.

No sooner had the recirculated draft made the rounds than Justice Frankfurter sent a terse note to the Conference enclosing his memorandum in *Knapp v. Schweitzer*, a 1958 case. Frankfurter's memo dated May 8, 1961, revealed his growing frustration at the developments he saw in *Mapp*. Having served on the Court for twenty-two years and nearly eighty years old, Frankfurter had little patience for even the discussion of overturning *Wolf*. "Herewith is a copy of my memorandum in *Knapp v. Schweitzer* which was offered as precedent for what is proposed to be done in *Mapp v. Ohio*. Res ipsa loquitur. [The facts speak for themselves.] As for the reliance on *Rogers v. Richmond*—I give up!" Five pages of typed memorandum followed.[28] The point of Frankfurter's writings is based on the principles of federalism. This case, like *Knapp v. Schweitzer*, presented nothing new for the Court to decide. To mandate exclusion upon the states is to reach out and answer a question that had been settled before. Any argument against settled doctrine was asking the Court to go beyond its scope and irresponsibly dictate criminal procedure to the states. Frankfurter's position, rooted in the philosophy of judicial restraint, was a dissent for Clark. He did not disagree about wording or phraseology, or additions or omissions to Clark's draft. His disagreement was on the very basis of the opinion itself. Clark must have realized that little would convince Frankfurter that *Wolf* should be undone and *Mapp* was the case to do it.

Harlan's dissent was also taking form, and by the end of May, Clark had a draft of his powerful statement. Stewart also indicated his departure from Clark's draft, yet it was only a half step. Stewart's May 31st letter to Clark

---

[28] As a trained political scientist, I particularly enjoyed Frankfurter's disdain for non-lawyerly analysis of legal issues. On page 3 he makes reference to articles by a Dr. Grant. He adds "Dr. Grant is a political scientist and not a lawyer, and like almost all political scientists who write on constitutional problems, even some of the best of them, like Dr. Corwin, they cavalierly disregard what to us lawyers is essential. The notion that Grant's articles should make us reverse the whole current of our constitutional law strikes me a bit odd." Box A115, Folder 6, Tom Clark Papers, Tarlton Law Library, The University of Texas at Austin, Austin, Texas.

indicated that he agreed with Part I of Justice Harlan's dissent. Here Harlan had forcefully stated that the majority in *Mapp* had "reached out" and turned an obvious case of statutory determination (the Ohio obscenity statute) into a constitutional issue concerning an issue that was raised only tangentially. Stewart went on to say that he made no decision on the merits of the issue decided by the Court and only concurred with Clark's opinion because he believed that the state statute violated petitioner's rights. Stewart's two-sentence concurrence gave Clark the necessary vote he needed but did little to lessen the controversy over the reach of the case. Harlan was a dissent, along with Frankfurter. But Stewart's narrow concurrence joined Warren, Brennan, Douglas, and Black to give Clark his majority. Stewart's draft was sent to the Court's in-house print shop and was circulated on June 3, 1961.

On June 5th Felix Frankfurter sent Clark a copy of the last page of Clark's draft in which he circled the notation: "Mr. Justice Frankfurter will in due course file a separate opinion." Frankfurter scrawled on the top: "Dear Tom: Please delete this. I'm joining John."[29] John, referring to Justice John Marshall Harlan, had recirculated his dissent on the 2nd of June and found agreement with Charley Whittaker and Frankfurter. Frankfurter had not officially joined and at the June 9th conference he gave Clark a handwritten note: "Tom: I'm very sorry to be holding up *Mapp* but it has nothing to do with your opinion or my desire and expectation to have it go down on Monday. FF." No doubt Frankfurter was bitter at losing the holding of *Wolf*. He would experience an even greater defeat before his retirement in the famous apportionment case of *Baker v. Carr. Mapp* no doubt was a sore spot.

The die was cast, and Clark's opinion would prevail. Knowing the numbers were there for Clark, both Justices Douglas and Black began to work on opinions that, while certainly not contradicting Clark, elaborated on their own positions and indicated their own assessment of the *Mapp* case. Douglas was

---

[29]   Box A115, Folder 6, Tom Clark Papers, Tarlton Law Library, The University of Texas at Austin, Austin, Texas.

in agreement concerning any First Amendment violation. However, he was willing to overrule *Wolf* very early on. An uncirculated draft dated April 3, 1961, revealed his strong sense that *Mapp* was indeed the vehicle for change. "I think it is time to overrule *Wolf v. Colorado*. I would apply the Fourth Amendment with full force to the States, making the exclusionary rule of the *Weeks* case part and parcel of the constitutional guarantee."[30] Douglas had sent his draft to Bill Brennan but felt no need to pursue it after seeing Clark's first draft, which achieved the same result. Indeed Douglas returned his copy of Clark's draft (sent to him on April 28th) on April 29th indicating his agreement.[31] By May 4th Douglas responded again to Clark with only stylistic changes. He wrote in the margin "I agree. WOD."[32] But now that Clark had his votes, Douglas telephoned him on June 2nd to indicate he was going to file something separately. Douglas began circulating a concurrence, which was essentially his earlier uncirculated draft. His additions were important because they reveal his concern for the controversy that *Mapp* would brew. Had the majority reached out to overrule *Wolf*? Douglas responded,

> I believe that this is an appropriate case in which to put an end to the asymmetry which *Wolf* imported into the law. It is an appropriate case because the facts it presents show—as would few other cases, the casual arrogance of those who have the untrammelled power to invade one's home and to seize one's person.

And to Frankfurter he added, "It is true that argument was mostly directed to another issue in this case, but that is often the fact. See *Rogers v. Richmond*, 365 U.S. 534, 535-540."[33] Douglas is referencing the early memo of May 8th

---

30   Box 62, File *"Mapp v. Ohio,"* William Brennan Papers, Library of Congress, Manuscript Room, Washington, D. C.

31   Box 1254, Folder, Misc, Memos, Cert Memos, William O. Douglas Papers, Library of Congress, Manuscript Room, Washington, D.C.

32   Recirculated draft of *Mapp v. Ohio*, Box A115, Folder 3, Tom Clark Papers, Tarlton Law Library, The University of Texas at Austin, Austin, Texas.

33   Ibid.

written by Frankfurter who was frustrated with the references to *Rogers*. When Frankfurter read Douglas's draft, he couldn't help but pen a retort. Douglas made the comment that the Wolf decision in 1949 had resulted in a storm of constitutional controversy that came to an end with the *Mapp* decision. Frankfurter sarcastically wrote in the margins of his copy, "I wonder in what Weather Bureau the 'storm' was recorded?"[34] Douglas's separate opinion focused entirely on the search and seizure issue raised in *Mapp*. His position strengthened Clark's opinion, arguing that for the Court to reach the Fourth Amendment issues was legitimate and in his mind necessary.

Black also began drafting a concurrence in *Mapp*. He agreed with Clark about the search and seizure violation and the support of the exclusionary rule, but used this opportunity to emphasize a coupling of the Fourth and Fifth Amendments. In his draft, circulated on June 6, 1961, he argued that "we definitely hold that the Fifth Amendment's protection against enforced self-incrimination and the Fourth Amendment's protections against unreasonable searches and seizures have both been extended to the states through the Fourteenth Amendment."[35] Citing *Boyd v. United States* (1886), which linked the exclusionary rule remedy to both the Fourth and Fifth Amendments, Black reached the same result. The search of Dollree Mapp's home was illegal. However, Black's legal reasoning caused Clark alarm.

On June 6th Clark wrote to Black, quoting back to Black his own language mentioned above. "As you know, I certainly would not wish you to change my statement of *your* understanding of the Court's opinion. In all fairness, however, as author of that opinion I must say...."[36] Clark explained his mention of the Fifth Amendment was only by way of analogy and he had no intention

---

[34]   Reel 67, Page 590, Felix Frankfurter Papers, Library of Congress Manuscript Room, Washington, D.C.

[35]   Draft of *Mapp v. Ohio* concurrence in Justice Black, in Box 349, Hugo Black Papers, Manuscript Room, Library of Congress, Washington, D. C.

[36]   Letter to Justice Black from Justice Clark, in Box 349, Hugo Black Papers, Manuscript Room, Library of Congress, Washington, D.C.

of inferring that the exclusionary rule proposed in *Mapp* had its roots in the Fifth Amendment. Clark's response to Black tailored the majority opinion in *Mapp* as only touching upon the Fourth Amendment. Clark most likely thought the matter was closed. However, Black had other concerns. As the term was winding down, Black wrote one more lengthy memorandum to Clark. Black's tone was serious and suggested that he needed clarification or he would change his vote. The date was June 15th and the term was to end the following day. Tom Clark must have felt his patience tried. His coalition was shifting, or so it appeared.

Black readily accepted Clark's explanation concerning the Fourth and Fifth Amendment and their supposed linkage. Just as Clark had believed, the matter was resolved. However, Black raised another issue, which may have been generated by the terse dissent of Justice Harlan.

> My agreement to your opinion depends upon my understanding that you read *Wolf* as having held, and that we are holding here, that the Fourth Amendment *as a whole* is applicable to the States and not some imaginary and unknown fragment designated as the "right of privacy." This understanding is one of the reasons I am willing to decide in this state case the question of the scope of the Fourth Amendment as applied to the Federal Government. If I am wrong in this and your opinion means that the Fourth Amendment does not apply to the States as a whole, I am unwilling to agree to decide this crucial question in this case and prefer to wait for a case that directly and immediately involves application of the Fourth Amendment to the Federal Government.[37]

At the eleventh hour, Hugo Black made it clear that the reach of *Mapp* was incorporating the remedy of exclusion in all cases of state search and seizure violations. Black's position on incorporation, applying the Bill of Rights to the states, had always been frustrated by the piecemeal approach of the Court, which he felt led to confusion and was essentially unfair. Black wanted to make

---

[37]   Memorandum from Justice Black to Justice Clark, found both in Box A115, Folder 6, Tom Clark Papers, Tarlton Law Library, University of Texas at Austin, Austin, Texas; and Box 349, Hugo Black Papers, Manuscript Room, Library of Congress, Washington, D.C.

sure that Fourth Amendment violations, whether at the hand of federal or state officials, would result in the automatic exclusion of the evidence. *Weeks* and *Mapp* would be the two cases that accomplished this result. Black made clear that if the scope and coverage of the Court's rulings were anything less, he would dissent and push for reargument as Harlan had suggested.

One can only imagine Clark's feelings at this late date. He had seen Douglas's concurrence and Stewart's as well. Harlan's dissent, joined by Whittaker as well as Frankfurter, had been received and even sent to the Court's print shop. The case was all but handed down. Black's note was immediately met with a response from Clark. In a one-sentence memo Clark wrote, "As to yours of June 15th, the gist of the opinion is that *Wolf* held the entire Fourth Amendment to be carried over against the states through the Fourteenth, and therefore the exclusionary rule which *Weeks* applied to federal cases must likewise be made applicable to state prosecutions."[38] Clark signed the brief response, "Very best, Tom." Black, apparently satisfied, remained with the majority.

On the eve of the historic decision being made public, it is interesting to note the path traveled by the *Mapp* case: Dollree Mapp's trial and conviction, the way she had lost every previous ruling, the way in which each court had found her violating the state statute. The only glimmer of hope lay in the interpretation that the state law making mere possession of obscene material a crime was overly broad and vague. Mapp's best chance at winning appeared to be in declaring the Ohio statute unconstitutional because of its reach. Yet on June 15, 1961, Clark's opinion made little mention of the Ohio obscenity statute. He was prepared to hand down the most important search and seizure decision in United States history. Neither Dollree Mapp nor Carl Delau could have known that their encounter in 1957 would end up making legal history.

At the Friday conference on June 16, 1961, Chief Justice Warren's "Agenda for the Conference" gave structure to the final public presentation of

---

[38]   Box 349, Hugo Black Papers, Library of Congress, Manuscript Room, Washington, D.C.

the 1960 Term. He began the conference by noting the proposed schedule for the 1961 term, which would begin in October. He also laid out the allotment of justices to the circuit courts over the summer break and even mentioned the summer vacation schedules of the justices as evident by his pencil mark notations in the upper right hand copy of his agenda.

Most important to the meeting was the list of opinions to be handed down on the final day of the term, June 19, 1961. By Monday the term would end. Fifth on the list of opinions was No. 236, *Mapp v. Ohio*. Justice Clark would deliver the court's opinion. Below Clark's name, Warren wrote in red pencil with small deliberate checks: Justice Douglas concurring, Justice Black concurring, Justice Harlan dissenting, Justice Stewart's Memo. Next to the docket number Warren had placed a large red "OK,"[39] indicating that the opinion was ready to be handed down on Opinion Monday, June 19, 1961. Clark's final version of *Mapp*, obviously the one sent to the printer, indicated where Clark had inserted the "19" in the space in June_,1961. In the corner he wrote, "OK. Mon."[40]

---

[39] Box 145, File OT1960(2), Earl Warren Papers, Manuscript Room, Library of Congress, Washington, D.C.

[40] Box A115, Folder 4, Tom Clark Papers, Tarlton Law Library, The University of Texas at Austin, Austin, Texas.

CHAPTER TEN

The Decision

Opinion Monday as it was called. More importantly, the last Opinion Monday of the term. Reporters for all the major news networks and wire services knew that all cases pending on the Court's docket would either be announced or carried over to the following term. After the public presentation on this mid-June day, the justices would not be in public session until the fall. They would disperse for the summer, most of them leaving the hot and humid confines of the nation's capital. Some of the justices traveled to exotic locations. Warren would spend some of the summer of 1961 globetrotting. Some would return to their home states, such as Douglas, who would see family and friends and hike his beloved mountains of the Pacific Northwest.

Warren's notes reflected his meticulous nature. After any admissions to the Supreme Court bar, the remaining opinions would be handed down. Next to each, Warren noted the time allotted to each case, beginning at 12:30 with No. 97 *Cafeteria and Restaurant Workers Union v. McElroy.* According to Warren's records, *Mapp v. Ohio* would be announced from the bench by Mr. Justice Clark beginning at 2:45 to 3:08 P.M., a span of just twenty-three minutes. Justice Harlan was allotted the nineteen minutes from 3:08 to 3:37 to explain his dissent.[1] Early enough to make the evening news cycle, but late enough to postpone any in-depth analysis, *Mapp v. Ohio* would be the most notable last-day decision of the high court.

For Carl Delau, now a sergeant on the Cleveland Police Force, June 19, 1961, was just like any other Monday. He paid little attention to the decisions

---

[1]   Earl Warren Papers, Library of Congress, Manuscript Room, Washington, D.C. See Photograph 5.

of the high court and only discovered the ruling when he read it in the newspaper the following day.[2] The event was not a significant one, in the sense that he was not waiting anxiously to receive word from the high bench. He had paid no attention to the Mapp litigation. In his mind, the case was an obscenity question regarding the Ohio statute litigated in *Lindway*. His search of Mapp's home and the seizure of the evidence was not the central issue. For Delau, *Mapp v. Ohio* was an obscenity case, nothing more. He had not followed the case through the court system. When asked to recall any news coverage about the Ohio Supreme Court decision or the oral arguments before the Supreme Court of the United States, Officer Delau could not.[3] For him, the case held no real salience, although that was to change. If asked about the Mapp case before June 19th, Delau would have said something like the following: "a known affiliate of local crime syndicates, Dollree Mapp, was clearly guilty of possessing obscene material." Little mention had been made about the search and seizure of Mapp's home, so Delau did not feel that his reputation was somehow being challenged. Only much later did the import of the decision have its full impact on him. Any defensiveness relating to the *Mapp* decision would come to a boil later.

Dollree Mapp, on the other hand, did watch the events in Washington with great interest. In an interview with the Cleveland *Call and Post*, she recounted her continual interest in the case. She and a girlfriend arrived by train in the nation's capital on an October day in 1960 to hear the oral arguments in her case. After finding a hotel that would accept blacks and taking in a few tourist

---

[2]   Interview with Carl I. Delau, 1995. Delau added an anecdote that Court watchers will find interesting. Delau knew Officer Marty McFadden, the police officer involved in another famous Cleveland search and seizure case, *Terry v. Ohio*, (1969). The two once discussed their fame or infamy, and both agreed that what occurred in Washington, while significant, felt remote at the time of the decision. Neither was "watching" the Court in anticipation of a decision. Delau and McFadden once traveled together to Washington, D.C., for police detail in the inaugural parade of Dwight D. Eisenhower.

[3]   Interview by the author with Carl I. Delau, October 2001.

attractions, she and her companion awoke the next day and went to the Supreme Court building. Dollree Mapp was in attendance for the oral arguments, seated in the public section of the courtroom, unbeknownst to the lawyers and justices. She told the *Call and Post* reporter that as she was leaving the courtroom at the conclusion of the oral argument, she met one of the doorkeepers and asked him when a decision was expected. He informed her that the Court often took months to decide cases. She then revealed to him that she was the litigant in the case just heard and that she was discouraged by the very long wait. She asked him if she could telephone him weekly to find out if there was a decision. He agreed. Each Monday she called. "Every Monday, I waited for the answer and they saved it until their very last session. I prayed for this! Then when it came, I fainted."[4]

The *Call and Post* article headlined her story, "Must Have Warrant Court Tells Police." Accompanying the article, on the front page, was a photograph of Dollree Mapp, smiling, joyful, her face upturned and her hands clasped indicating her victory was sweet indeed. In her interview with the reporter, Bob Williams, Mapp sounded sophisticated and worldly, yet vulnerable. "I was in Kentucky on another case when my lawyers said they had a telephone call on the Supreme Court case. I had prayed for the answer that came, but when they told me the court had reversed my conviction, I just couldn't take it. The next thing I knew, they were reviving me. It has been four years of torture and uncertainty."[5] The article was one of vindication for Mapp, always described as the "nationally known former wife of ex-boxer Jimmy Bivins and former girl friend of Archie Moore, light heavyweight boxing champion."[6] Her future press clippings would not be so laudatory, but for now the limelight shone warmly on her. She was beautiful, a flashy dresser, and her dramatic interviewing flair made for good press. The Court decision placed her center stage. Her name

---

[4]   *Call and Post*, June 24, 1961, p. 1.

[5]   Ibid., p. 2A.

[6]   Ibid., p. 1.

would become synonymous with other landmark Court rulings such as *Miranda, Gideon,* and *Escobedo*. Any first-year law student knows of the plight of Ernesto Miranda, Clarence Earl Gideon, and Danny Escobedo. So too do they know the name Dollree Mapp. Mapp joined this group of infamous litigants, giving face to a landmark Supreme Court ruling that even in 2004 enjoys widespread notoriety.[7] While her feeling of exhilaration dominated this particular Monday in June of 1961, she would later state that the decision and its accompanying fame created severe penalties for her.[8]

The opinion was reported in all the major newspapers around the country, usually on the front page. The *Cleveland Plain Dealer* led with the headline "Local Case Upsets Laws of Evidence." The *Plain Dealer* seemed more intrigued by the obscenity charge and the famous connections of Miss Mapp than the core ruling in the case. Calling her a "confidante of numbers racketeers, former wife of Jimmy Bivens, the boxer, and onetime friend of Archie Moore, the light heavyweight boxing champion,"[9] the article went on to explain her conviction on the state obscenity charge. Indeed, as the story continued on to the inside of the newspaper, the secondary heading read: "Smut Ruling."[10] Mapp's attorney was quoted as claiming only partial victory, having

---

[7]   One of the foremost websites for Court watchers is oyez. Here one can find a synopsis of a Supreme Court opinion detailing the reasoning of the Court and the vote of each justice. In addition, the site provides copies of transcripts of the decision, briefs, and the oral arguments. Some cases include an audio transcription of the Court's hearing of the case. Oyez lists its "top ten" most requested cases. *Mapp v. Ohio* is one of them.

[8]   Interview with Dollree Mapp, March 15, 1993. Later Mapp was arrested and convicted for narcotics possession. She was sentenced to twenty years to life. "It was a frame. I wouldn't be here if I wasn't black and I wasn't the Mapp in *Mapp vs. Ohio*," she told reporters. See "Six Defendants Whose Cases Changed American Law," *People Magazine*, May 5, 1975, pp. 14-15.

[9]   *Cleveland Plain Dealer*, June 20, 1961, p. 1A.

[10] Ibid., p. 5A.

hoped that the U.S. Supreme Court would overrule the *Lindway* decision and declare the Ohio obscenity statute unconstitutional. [11]

The *New York Times* gave the decision front page space on June 20, 1961, devoting much of the article to restating the major Fourth Amendment issues. "High Court Bars Evidence States Seize Illegally" was the headline. Little mention was made of the obscenity issue. The focus was overwhelmingly upon the *Wolf-Mapp* nexus and its impact on state criminal law. Russell Baker, the writer, argued that the case may be "the most significant limitation ever imposed on state criminal procedure by the Supreme Court in a single decision."[12] It was a bit unusual for the Court to overrule a previous decision, but all the more unusual given that the briefs and oral arguments did not focus on search and seizure, noted the *Times*. The *Times* reprinted Clark's majority opinion and excerpts of the Harlan dissent and the memorandum of Stewart.

An analysis followed the next day. The insightful writer Anthony Lewis, who would later pen the book *Gideon's Trumpet*, about another famous criminal procedure case, *Gideon v. Wainwright*, wrote a detailed analysis of the *Mapp* decision. Having witnessed the oral arguments, Lewis focused on the broader issue of incorporation. In his article, "An Old Court Dispute," Lewis viewed the *Mapp* case through the lense of the chronic legal dispute of incorporation. If this provision of the Bill of Rights was applied to the states, eliminating their choice of Fourth Amendment remedies (now it must be exclusion), what other portions of the Bill of Rights would be subject to the same application? Wondered Lewis, "The question is what this (*Mapp v. Ohio*) signifies for issues aside from search and seizure."[13]

---

[11]   Ibid., p. 5A.

[12]   "High Court Bars Evidence States Seized Illegally," *New York Times*, June 20, 1961, p. 1A.

[13]   Anthony Lewis, "An Old Court Dispute," *New York Times*, June 21, 1961, p. 21A.

Lewis's eye was keen indeed, for the decade of the 1960s would see the Fifth Amendment self-incrimination[14] and double jeopardy clauses,[15] the Sixth Amendment right to counsel,[16] confrontation of witnesses,[17] speedy trial,[18] and trial by jury[19] provisions, and the Eighth Amendment protection against cruel and unusual punishment[20] all applied to state criminal proceedings in identical fashion as in federal ones. *Mapp* was the first of this criminal procedure revolution. By the time Earl Warren left the high bench in 1969, little of the Bill of Rights criminal procedure provisions remained differentiated in state and federal courts.

Neither the Vinson Court before him nor the Burger Court after him would have the impact the Warren Court justices did on criminal procedure. In terms of rights of the accused, *Mapp* was the beginning of the due process revolution. The five to four ruling caught law enforcement off guard. What had been acceptable practice prior to the Mapp search in 1957 was no more. The legal community too was stunned by the Court's reach. *Wolf* had indicated that states must set standards for meeting the threshold of Fourth Amendment due process. *Mapp* altered the tone. Criminal procedure safeguards were in the hands of the Supreme Court. Furthermore, replaying the *Mapp* decision throughout the decade in terms of Fifth, Sixth, and Eighth Amendment rights left police reeling, state legislatures gasping, and the legal community uncertain

---

14   *Malloy v. Hogan*, 378 U.S. 1 (1964). Also clarifying state criminal procedure is *Murphy v. Waterfront Commission of New York Harbor*, 387 U.S. 52 (1964) and *Miranda v. Arizona* 384 U.S. 436 (1966).

15   *Benton v. Maryland*, 359 U.S. 784 (1969).

16   *Gideon v. Wainwright*, 372 U.S. 335 (1963).

17   *Pointer v. Texas*, 380 U.S. 300 (1965). See also *Washington v. Texas*, 388 U.S.14 (1967) concerning the compulsory process to obtain witnesses.

18   *Klopfer v. North Carolina*, 386 U.S. 213 (1967).

19   *Duncan v. Louisiana*, 391 U.S. 145 (1968).

20   *Robinson v. California*, 370 U.S. 660 (1962).

about the role of courts in instituting rapid and complete change in what had been a traditional state function, criminal law.[21]

The *Times* article surmised that "the search and seizure decision is expected to have sweeping effects on local law enforcement throughout the country."[22] Given the reaction of those in law enforcement around the nation, the media had keenly gauged their temperature. By July 2, 1961, the District Attorney's Association of the State of New York called on Governor Rockefeller to join them in seeking to overturn the decision in *Mapp v. Ohio*. One reason given was that the high court ruling would weaken the effectiveness of law enforcement to combat illegal narcotics trafficking.[23] In August 1961 the *New York Times* reported procedural changes in St. Louis due to lost arrests as a result of the *Mapp* decision.[24] The Court of Appeals in Albany New York attempted to establish a policy on the application of the *Mapp* decision on cases pending on the docket. The court in adopting the policy admitted "it would likely result in the reversal of many convictions in pending cases."[25] Across the country, judges and police chiefs tried to sort out what *Mapp* meant in terms of the legitimacy of current police practices. What kinds of changes were necessary and which would pass constitutional muster? Clearly, guidance was needed, and shortly after *Mapp* the Court would clarify the application of the exclusionary rule to a bevy of scenarios. The docket in 1962 and each year thereafter reflected this wave. But before the aftermath of the Mapp decision is laid out in terms of Supreme Court doctrine, it must be said that not all the

---

[21] All the incorporation cases contributed to the overall change in terms of pragmatic and philosophical application of criminal procedure. However, *Mapp* in 1961, taken together with *Gideon* in 1963 and *Miranda* in 1966, would do much to revamp the criminal justice system. These three pillars of criminal procedure would change the very meaning of criminal justice in the United States.

[22] "High Court Bars Evidence States Seized Illegally," *New York Times*, June 20, 1961, p. 1A.

[23] *New York Times*, July 2, 1961, p. 24A.

[24] *New York Times*, August 6, 1961, p. 30A.

[25] *New York Times*, December 1, 1961, p. 21A.

reactions to *Mapp* were negative or even tentative. Even the personal correspondence of the justices reflected support and affirmation of a ruling that some felt was long overdue.

The Supreme Court papers of Justices Clark, Douglas, and Black all contain letters and clippings sent from prominent members of state bars, law schools and the like, hailing the ruling. For example, on July 7, 1961, Justice Clark received a letter from John P. Frank, a well known legal scholar and attorney (who sent a carbon to Justice Black) stating: "In my own writings for thirteen years, I have always said that I felt that the *Wolf* case was a sorry example of intellectualism gone mad—a resolution of a problem right in principle but utterly wrong in practical application. And so I am one of those who is tremendously pleased with your recent opinion."[26] Justice Black received correspondence from Louis H. Pollak, a noted law professor and former clerk of Justice Rutledge, on June 26, 1961, in which he said, "I have just read, with great pleasure, your very thoughtful and persuasive concurring opinion in *Mapp v. Ohio*."[27] Pollak then went on to explain that Justice Rutledge's dissent in *Wolf v. Colorado* was one of the last opinions penned by the justice before his death. Black's opinion in *Mapp*, similar in vein to Rutledge's *Wolf* opinion would have, in Pollak's mind, been for Justice Rutledge "a source of great gratification."[28] Three days later Black responded with a kind reply.[29]

Justice Douglas wrote a letter to Justice Clark, which he also copied to the rest of the Brethren, recounting the reaction of the California Attorney General, Stanley Mosk, to the *Mapp* decision. According to Douglas, at a social event the attorney general approached him and "out of the blue he commented,

---

[26]   Tom Clark Papers, Tarlton Law Library, The University of Texas at Austin , Austin, Texas.

[27]   Hugo Black Papers, Library of Congress, Manuscript Room, Washington, D.C.

[28]   Ibid.

[29]   Ibid.

'Thank the good Lord for *Mapp v. Ohio*.'[30] Douglas went on to explain the context of the comment, a high-profile California case in which the media attention created pressure on elected judges to try to find a way around the Fourth Amendment. "The result of *Mapp v. Ohio*, according to Mosk, is to take the pressure off the local judges to create exceptions and to follow the exclusionary rule and all its ramifications."[31] This comment drew a response from Frankfurter that was more a condemnation of the attitude that federal intervention is necessary in resolving state problems, the thorny problem of federalism, rather than on the merits of the *Mapp* holding. Frankfurter even went so far as to write to Douglas, "Dear Bill: When next you see Attorney General Mosk please ask him if California was not "in the Union" before June 19, 1961. Sincerely yours, F.F."[32] *Mapp* appeared to be the segue for a dialogue on other contentious issues, in its own way, a lightning rod.

Reaction to *Mapp* even appeared in the *Congressional Record*. In a dramatic statement by the Honorable James C. Healy of New York on February 3, 1964, the congressman quoted from the speech of a constituent, Howard Goldfluss, to the Bronx Rotary Club:

> Since 1961, the hue and cry of the good guys [his label for state attorney's general, district attorneys, county prosecutors, and police departments] has come to nothing. The police officers are doing now what they should have been compelled to do all these years; securing a warrant before violating the sanctity of a man's home.[33]

---

[30] Letter dated January 25, 1962, Box 351, File "Correspondence with WOD," Earl Warren Papers, Library of Congress, Manuscript Room, Washington, D.C.

[31] Letter dated January 25, 1962. William O. Douglas Papers, Library of Congress, Manuscript Room, Washington, D.C.

[32] Memorandum to the Conference dated January 31, 1962. William O. Douglas Papers, Library of Congress, Manuscript Room, Washington, D.C..

[33] *Congressional Record*, Appendix, February 3, 1964, p. A490. Reproduced in the Hugo Black Papers, Manuscript Room, Library of Congress, Washington, D.C.

He continued, "Statistics show that since the *Mapp* case there has been no significant proportional change in the amount of convictions nationwide."[34] Goldfluss sent a copy of the *Congressional Record* to Justice Black, thanking the justice for his preservation of Fourth Amendment rights in his *Mapp* opinion.

Whereas the initial reaction by law enforcement and state governments may have been one of shock, the justices were generally left with the impression that *Mapp* was a good decision in the long run. Adjustments had been made and the implementation of *Mapp* was rough in transition but not unworkable. The reaction, however, did create more work for the Brethren. No sooner had they decided *Mapp* than they were asked to interpret the details of the exclusionary rule. Was *Mapp* a bright line rule? Would evidence always be excluded if there was deemed a Fourth Amendment violation? Were there times when it was impractical to expect police to obtain warrants before searching, for example, during regular street encounters or circumstances of exigency? Should the Court apply *Mapp* retroactively, meaning to individuals who were searched and evidence against them was seized without a warrant before June 19, 1961? These questions came in the form of litigation, volumes of it. The justices found themselves with a steady diet of state appeals asking them to spell out the details of Fourth Amendment law.

One hundred and seventy years after the adoption of the Fourth Amendment, the Supreme Court of the United States in *Mapp v. Ohio* required exclusion in state cases. On the eve of that decision, most English-language jurisdictions still rejected the approach of Weeks.[35] *Linkletter v. Walker*[36] and

---

34   Ibid., p. A491.

35   Some states such as New York, New Jersey, and Massachusetts tried immediately to implement the exclusionary rule because of the *Mapp* ruling. Others, Pennsylvania for example, evaded the force of *Mapp*. See David R. Manwaring, "The Impact of *Mapp v. Ohio*." Unpublished paper delivered at 1964 Annual Meeting of the American Political Science Association Convention, Chicago, Illinois, September 9-12, 1964. Cited in Jacob Landynski, *Search and Seizure and the Supreme Court: A Study in Constitutional*

Angelet v. Fay,[37] denied relief against state convictions finalized before the overruling of *Wolf.* In other words, the remedy of exclusion would not be applied retroactively. This suggested somewhat less than full enthusiasm for exclusion even among the Warren Court justices. If the remedy of exclusion was part of the Fourth Amendment guarantee, it seemed logical and consistent to award the protection to both pre- and post-*Mapp* convictions. The impact would be enormous. Retrials would be required in many cases, this time with the omission of evidence produced by an illegal search and seizure. In others, convicted criminals would be released, since the burden of due process required a new look at any taint to evidence, evidence that may have long ago disappeared from police storage rooms.

Justice Clark, *Mapp's* author, wrote the opinion in *Linkletter v. Walker*, ruling against extending the exclusionary rule to cases decided before *Mapp.* The premise of the exclusionary rule, to deter police misconduct and to preserve the integrity of the judiciary were well stated and reasoned in *Mapp.* However, Clark here pigeonholed his rationale. In *Linkletter* he reasoned that if the exclusionary rule was to deter police misconduct, little would be gained by applying the rule to police officers searching before the rule was stipulated. The misconduct had already occurred and Mapp's exclusionary rule was to *prevent* misconduct, not remedy that which had already taken place.[38] *Linkletter* narrowed the scope of the exclusionary rule and blurred its very existence. If the exclusionary rule was a constitutionally required remedy, was it not then a

---

Interpretation (Baltimore: The Johns Hopkins University Press, 1966), p. 193, n. 93.

[36]   381 U.S. 618 (1965). Speedy justice did not serve Linkletter well. The search and seizure he was subjected to occurred on August 16, 1958; Ms. Mapp's on May 23, 1957. His case was decided before Mapp's even though the police conduct in question occurred later than that of Mapp. The end result is that the exclusionary rule protected Mapp from her 1957 search and seizure but found any misconduct in Linkletter's 1958 situation without such a remedy.

[37]   381 U.S. 654 (1965).

[38]   381 U.S. 618 (1965).

remedial requirement for all? If it was not constitutionally required, inherent
in the Fourth Amendment right, then logically it was judicially created. If so,
the exclusionary rule was then subject to a future of judicial and potentially
legislative interpretation. The implications of *Linkletter* were damning. The
Court appeared, in the person of Tom Clark himself, to contradict the rationale
and justification of the *Mapp* holding.[39]

Indeed Chief Justice Warren commented on behalf of the Court in *Terry v.
Ohio:* "I see that the exclusionary rule has its limitations as a tool of judicial
control. In some contexts the rule is ineffective as a deterrent, given the wide
diversity in street encounters between citizens and police."[40] The exclusionary
rule, seemingly a "bright line" one, would be subject to the interpretations of
"context" as the Chief mentioned. The diversity of encounter between the
citizenry and law enforcement would lead to the eventual creation of rules and
exceptions to make the exclusionary rule pragmatically workable. For example,
the much-heralded *Terry* decision in which Warren made his above-mentioned
comment, focused on the reasonableness of stopping a suspicious individual
without a warrant, yet allowing the incriminating evidence to be admissible in
court.[41]

A high volume of litigation produced many exceptions to the requirement
of a search warrant. The basis of these exceptions was that they are reasonable.
The most common searches in the United States, searches after arrest, were
allowed to be conducted without search warrants because the justices concluded

---

[39]   The Sixth Amendment guarantee of the right to counsel was treated altogether differently
        by the Court. *Gideon v. Wainwright* mandated the right to counsel in felony cases and was
        applied retroactively. The impact in Florida alone, the state of Gideon's original trial, was
        enormous. Nevertheless, the Court held fast to the constitutional status of a right to counsel.
        Some retreats would follow but not with regard to earlier litigants.

[40]   392 U.S. 1, 8 (1968).

[41]   See *Terry v. Ohio*, 392 U.S. 1 (1968). In the fall of 2003 the City of Cleveland placed a
        marker on the downtown street corner to commemorate the scene of the famous "Terry stop"
        of Officer Mary McFadden.

it was reasonable for arresting officers to secure any evidence suspects might have on their person and moreover, to ensure the safety of the police officer. Exceptions from the search warrant requirement were allowed for border searches, administrative searches, and logically, when the individual consented voluntarily to be searched. The justices wrestled with the particulars of automobile searches, allowing a generalized exception to the warrant requirement to stop an automobile but unsure about the status of the glove box, the trunk, and items inside the body of a vehicle. Did a search include the area surrounding an individual, that "under their immediate control"? Could a police officer search without a warrant when in "hot pursuit" of an individual? The justices took each of these questions, case by case, using what Justice Clark would term a "common sense" approach. The Court became a national review board, defining police procedure piecemeal. Those in charge of training and education in the nation's police academies found themselves regularly digesting the latest search and seizure opinion from the high bench and trying to understand it in terms of its implications to the cop on the beat.

As New York City Police Commissioner Michael Murphy put it, police departments had to "adopt new policies and new instructions. Retraining sessions had to be held from the very top administrators down to each of the thousands of foot patrolmen and detectives engaged in the daily enforcement function."[42] In Cleveland, a Warrant Registry Office was established in the Detective Bureau on May 1, 1961. The purpose of the registry was to provide the arresting officer with detailed information that would be useful in the execution of a warrant. From May 1, 1961, to December 31, 1961, 1,630 warrants were registered under this new system and 1,359 actually executed. The impact of the *Mapp* decision on police departments involved was profound.[43] By 1965 the Cleveland Police Academy reported the breakdown of

---

[42]   Michael Murphy, "Judicial Review of Police Methods in Law Enforcement: The Problem of Compliance by Police Departments," 44 *Texas Law Review* 941 (1966).

[43]   1961 Annual Report of the Cleveland Police Department.

class work and training for new recruits. Ten hours were spent on vice, policy, and gambling. Sixteen hours were spent on the rules of evidence.[44]

Amid the ensuing litigation generated by the *Mapp* ruling, the justices were also faced with the particular appeal by the state of Ohio, asking them to reconsider their decision in *Mapp v. Ohio*. The petition filed by the state was as expected. Ohio argued that a rehearing should be granted to adequately allow them to argue the search and seizure issues of the case and the impact of incorporating the exclusionary rule and applying it to state governments. Two "friends of the court" briefs, amicus curiae, were filed by the National District Attorneys' Association and the state of California (asking particularly about the reach of *Mapp v. Ohio* in light of controversial and high profile cases). The California petition contained questions that the Court would inevitably have to address: "Whether the same standards of reasonableness applicable to federal officers under the Fourth Amendment will be applied to state officers? Whether a defendant can be compelled to raise the question prior to trial? Is *Mapp* retrospective?" As is common in requests for rehearing, Warren's clerk recommended denying the petition on the grounds that it raised no question the Court had not considered in the first case. The court ultimately denied the petition for rehearing and the case of *Mapp v. Ohio* was dispensed from the Supreme Court docket.[45]

On March 2, 1962, the clerk of the Court of Common Pleas in Cuyahoga County, Emil J. Masgay, received a letter from John F. Davis, the clerk of the Supreme Court of the United States. Attached with Davis's letter was the original record of *Mapp v. Ohio* when the Supreme Court had noted probable jurisdiction and accepted the appeal from the Ohio Supreme Court. Davis,

---

[44]   1965 Annual Report of the Cleveland Police Department.

[45]   Petition for Rehearing/Conference Memos/Bench Memos, Box 210, Earl Warren Papers, Library of Congress Manuscript Room, Washington, D.C.

actually his assistant, W. M. Allison, requested that Masgay acknowledge receipt, which no doubt he did.[46]

---

[46]   Handwritten on the docket sheet of *Mapp v. Ohio* is the notation, "March 5, 1962 C of A File [Court of Appeal File], B of X [Box of Evidence] and Original Papers returned from U.S. Supreme Court." Docket sheets for *Mapp v. Ohio*, Court of Common Pleas, Court of Appeals 8th District, microfilm, Court of Common Pleas, August 12, 1992.

CHAPTER ELEVEN
The Aftermath

I am expected to have the courage of an astronaut, the chivalry of Sir Walter Raleigh, the integrity of George Washington, the judgment of a Supreme Court Justice, the patience and restrain of a Sunday school teacher, and the sweetness and light of a saint.
—John T. Corrigan in *Blue Line*, a monthly law enforcement publication June 20, 1971

Even though the Supreme Court of the United States was through with the legal trial of Dollree Mapp, it was far from finished with interpreting the Fourth Amendment. On average the Court docket contained at least ten cases per term turning on Fourth Amendment grounds. Clearly *Mapp* had not laid down a bright-line rule. The Warren Court, then the Burger and Rehnquist Courts were left to line draw the particulars of search and seizure law. Technology, both in terms of crime fighting and criminal activity, and legal creativity added to the volume. However, instead of broadening the scope of the exclusionary rule and Fourth Amendment application, the Court took a different tack.

Something of a counterrevolution in search and seizure law began with the ascent of Chief Justice Warren E. Burger. Appointed by Richard Nixon to replace Earl Warren, Burger appeared to satisfy Nixon's litmus test of a "strict constructionist," meaning one who would remain within the confines of the Constitution and fight the urge to continually revisit the scope of current constitutional doctrine. In *Bivens v. Six Unknown Named Agents of the Federal Bureau of Narcotics,*[1] the Court responded to a major defect in *Weeks-Mapp* by

---

[1]   403 U.S. 388 (1971).

creating a new remedy for innocent victims of improper searches, holding negligent police officers civilly liable under 42 United States Code, Section 1983. The remedy of exclusion was only applicable to those who had something to exclude. Wrongfully searched individuals had little recourse. The *Bivens* ruling provided an avenue. In *Harris v. New York*,[2] the Court upheld the admission of illegally obtained evidence to impeach the credibility of the accused who testified in his own defense. This reaffirmed a Warren Court principle with regard to truth seeking in trial courts.[3] Individuals who took the witness stand and lied could expect tainted evidence to enter into trial to indicate their perjury to the jury. *United States v. Havens*[4] further allowed the use of illegally seized evidence against the accused to impeach his or her honesty. Then came then *United States v. Calandra*,[5] which rejected the extension of the exclusionary rule in grand jury proceedings. Next *United States v. Janis*[6] rejected exclusion in federal civil proceedings involving evidence improperly seized by state lawmen.

The great blow came in *Stone v. Powell*,[7] which clearly denied the exclusionary rule any supposed constitutional status. It is merely, the Court said, "a judicially created remedy or sanction against police misconduct rather than a personal constitutional right of the accused."[8] The implication, of course, was that it could be abolished by legislation. Moreover, without constitutional status, it would have to stand or fall on the court's estimate of its value "in the light of competing policies." In making that estimate the justices reviewed some of the rule's difficulties (beyond those mentioned herein above):

---

[2] 401 U.S. 222 (1971).

[3] See *Walder v. United States*, 347 U.S. 62 (1954).

[4] 446 U.S. 620 (1980).

[5] 414 U.S. 338 (1974).

[6] 428 U.S. 433 (1976).

[7] 428 U.S. 465 (1976).

[8] 428 U.S. 465, 489 (1976).

The costs of applying the exclusionary rule even at trial and on direct review are well known: the focus of the trial, and the attention of the participants therein, are diverted from the ultimate question of guilt or innocence that should be the central concern in a criminal proceeding. Moreover, the physical evidence sought to be excluded is typically reliable and often the most probative information bearing on the guilt or innocence of the defendant. Application of the rule thus deflects the truth finding process and often frees the guilty. The disparity in particular cases between the error committed by the police officer and the windfall afforded a guilty defendant by application of the rule is contrary to the ideal of proportionality that is essential to the concept of justice. Thus, although the rule is thought to deter unlawful police activity in part through the nurturing of respect for Fourth Amendment values, if applied indiscriminately it may well have the opposite effect of generating disrespect for the law and administration of justice. These long-recognized costs of the rule persist when a criminal conviction is sought to be overturned on collateral review on the ground that a search and seizure claim was erroneously rejected by two or more tiers of state courts.[9]

Weighing such costs against the supposed deterrent value of exclusion in habeas corpus (as distinct from direct) review, the Court found the cost prohibitive. Again exclusion was much diminished as a Fourth Amendment remedy.

Another blow came in *Nix v. Williams*,[10] which held that, "[W]hen the evidence in question would inevitably have been discovered without reference to the police error or misconduct, there is no nexus between the error and the evidence sufficient to provide a taint and the evidence is admissible."[11] The rationale for this "inevitable discovery" rule was that, given society's need for reliable evidence of an offender's guilt, the need to deter police misbehavior is adequately satisfied if offending police are put in the position they would have enjoyed had the misbehavior not occurred. Whereas the Warren Court was concerned about police misconduct, the Burger Court seemed to take an

---

[9]   428 U.S. 465, 489-1 (1976).

[10]   104 U.S. 3405 (1984).

[11]   Ibid.

approach of balance. The Court seemed to weigh the exclusion and lost arrest/conviction with the deterrence of police misbehavior. What emerged was no overarching principle, but a case-by-case balancing test.

The drift of the exceptions to exclusion seemed clear. *Linkletter, Angelet, Harris, Calandra, Havens, Janis, Stone*, and *Nix* marked a path back to Madison and the writing of the Fourth Amendment. Clearly, the Supreme Court had searched to find a firm foundation in the text, principles, and history of the Fourth Amendment. They reached a decision through their discretionary docket, well over two hundred cases touching upon the breadth and scope of the amendment. The justices may have forgotten that the abusive use of the general warrant rather than excessive zeal by "unreasonable" police led to the creation of the Fourth Amendment. By now, it appeared, the Fourth Amendment stood on its head. As Justice Black so aptly put it in the case *Davis v. Mississippi*, "this Court has been so widely blowing up the Fourth Amendment's scope that its original authors would be hard put to recognize their creation."[12]

~~~

On the eve of even bigger changes to the Fourth Amendment, several justices began to voice publicly their opinion on the Warren Court remedy of exclusion. For three evenings in April 1983, Justice Potter Stewart, the writer of the memorandum opinion in *Mapp*, spoke at Columbia University Law School, delivering what was known as the Harlan Fiske Stone Lecture series. The series was held in honor of the former Chief Justice, who had also served as the dean of Columbia School of Law. Stewart's lecture was entitled, "The Road to *Mapp v. Ohio* and Beyond: The Origins, Development and Future of the Exclusionary Rule in Search and Seizure Cases." Stewart, who retired from the Court in 1981, explained the selection of his topic.

---

[12]   89 S. Ct. 1394, 1399 (1969).

I have selected as the topic of these lectures an area in which the question of 'what the law used to be' requires an analysis of almost a hundred years of case law in this country and literally hundreds of years of history; (pause) in which the question 'what is the law now' can be answered only with as complex a delineation of rules, exceptions and refinements as exists in any field of jurisprudence (pause); and in which the question 'what should the law be in the future' is currently a subject of heated debate among members of the executive, legislative and judicial branches of the federal government and among concerned state and local government officials and members of the public as well.[13]

Stewart then set forth the facts of the *Mapp* case in a straightforward fashion. He noted that the case was in essence a First Amendment one and that at the time Clark was assigned to write the opinion, the substance of the case turned on the Ohio obscenity statute. He then stated that while he did not have exact knowledge, he concluded that the *Mapp* majority met in what he called a "rump caucus" to discuss a different tack for the case. He surmised that this was how *Mapp*, a First Amendment case, was converted to one of Fourth Amendment interpretation. "My reaction when Tom Clark's proposed Court opinion reached my desk was complete shock."[14]

Stewart then went on to present an in-depth historical analysis of *Mapp*, recounting many of the developments detailed in chapter four of this book. Despite his earlier shock. Stewart concluded the first evening's lecture by saying "I for one believe there is today and always has been a strong basis of support for the rule that unconstitutionally seized evidence is inadmissible against a defendant in a criminal trial."[15] For him, the *Mapp* case was the improper vehicle for such a change but the outcome was a just one. He left listeners with the notion that perhaps in the next two lectures he would criticize yet ultimately defend the decision in *Mapp*.

---

[13]   Potter Stewart, Harlan Fiske Stone Lectures, Lecture April 26, 1983, Columbia Law School, Transcript, p. 2-3.

[14]   Ibid., pp. 8-9.

[15]   Ibid., p. 31.

The judicially moderate Stewart, who could not bring himself in 1961 to support Clark's decision, argued philosophically about the cyclical nature of law and the long-term benefits of the outcome in *Mapp*. He detailed several possible rationales for exclusion as the remedial answer to the Fourth Amendment. It is interesting to note that while supporting the exclusionary rule, Justice Stewart did not view the rule as a constitutional requirement. He argued in his presentation that the history of the amendment's language and the doctrinal development mandated a remedy, but not necessarily any particular one. Whereas Justice Black linked the Fifth Amendment's exclusionary rule logically to the Fourth (much like Justice Day in *Boyd v. United States*) Stewart saw no such parallel. He argued that "the Constitution requires only that there be some *effective* remedy to ensure that agents of the government obey the Fourth Amendment. Thus exclusion is constitutionally required only if, without it, there would be no adequate means to ensure that the government obeys the Fourth Amendment."[16] Stewart's approach reflected the case law that had transpired since the 1961 decision, and it should be noted that Stewart was generally in the majority on the post-*Mapp* cases that came before him.[17] The exclusionary rule did not have constitutional status. Stewart even went so far as to argue that "as the threat to those liberties guaranteed by the Fourth Amendment changes, so also must the focus of the courts' inquiry into the adequacy of remedies for violations of those liberties."[18] In other words, the remedy of exclusion could at some point be replaced by other more effective remedies given a changing world. Stewart discussed other remedies such as civil action against police officers but found each limited in its utility in

---

[16]   Potter Stewart, Harlan Fiske Stone Lectures, Lecture April 27, 1983, Columbia Law School, Transcript, p. 23.

[17]   Stewart's most remembered Fourth Amendment case came in *Katz v. United States* in 1967. Writing for an eight-to-one majority, Stewart applied the warrant requirement to wiretapping, arguing that "The Fourth Amendment protects people not places." Even in a public telephone booth citizens had a right to privacy, free from governmental intrusion.

[18]   Stewart, Lecture, 1983, p. 25.

securing Fourth Amendment rights. Stewart concluded that the exclusionary rule was part of our culture and was the best choice available for providing remedial relief to the greatest number of victims of illegal searches and seizures. The exclusionary rule was constitutionally required, as the majority in *Mapp* argued. His case memorandum, generated because the Court decided an issue it was not asked to consider, did not mean that he did not agree that the exclusionary rule was necessary for Fourth Amendment protection.[19]

Stewart also made the very important point that the impact of the *Mapp* decision has been one of professionalizing policing in the United States. He quoted the former New York City deputy police commissioner, Leonard Reisman, who stated that before *Mapp*, "nobody bothered to take out search warrants." Up until *Mapp*, the Supreme Court did not exclude the evidence (remember *Irvine*?) "So the feeling was [about obtaining search warrants] why bother?"[20] Carl Delau argued this very point in defending his actions in searching Dollree Mapp. The norm was to not obtain a warrant. The Court saw the issue differently, ruled differently, and police now acted differently on the street. The change was by and large for the better.

The remaining question was: had the Supreme Court gone too far in its development of search and seizure law since *Mapp*? Stewart conceded in his final lecture, entitled "The Fate of the Exclusionary Rule," that the price of exclusion, the loss of probative and tangible evidence, was sometimes tragically high. It provided a windfall to the guilty, whether the individual had committed petty burglary or murder.[21] But to abolish the rule required an alternative that would meet the constitutional mandate of the Fourth Amendment.[22] To lessen the reach of the exclusionary rule was also to

---

[19]   Ibid., pp. 30-33.

[20]   Quoted in Ibid., pp. 25-26.

[21]   Potter Stewart, Harlan Fiske Stone Lectures, Lecture April 28, 1983, Columbia Law School, Transcript, pp. 12-16.

[22]   Stewart noted that in the 97th and 98th Congresses legislation was introduced to eliminate the exclusionary rule and replace it with a tort remedy, allowing Fourth Amendment victims

jeopardize Fourth Amendment guarantees unless a viable alternative remedy was adopted. Stewart saved his most biting criticism for the latest attempt to limit the exclusionary rule's impact, the good faith exception. Simply stated, the good faith argument supported the admissibility of tainted evidence if it was obtained under a reasonable belief that the search was lawful under the Fourth Amendment. The goal of deterring police misconduct was not served if the police behavior reflected the officer's belief that at the time he was acting lawfully. Stewart argued against such an exception, but none of his points seemed persuasive.[23] A keen read indicates that Stewart knew the inevitability of good faith. The Supreme Court, given its recent decisions, would most likely adopt it.

The idea of a good faith exception was debated in the halls of Congress, in the academic literature, and in legal circles. Even the president of the United States criticized the exclusionary rule. In a speech to the International Association of Chiefs of Police, President Ronald Reagan said of the rule, "this rule rests on the absurd proposition that a law enforcement error, no matter how technical, can be used to justify throwing an entire case out of court, no matter how guilty the defendant or how heinous the crime."[24] The exclusionary rule was a tempting target for all politicians campaigning on law-and-order tickets. Crime was a major problem and the police should not be "handcuffed" by a rule that served no purpose. If the goal of excluding probative evidence was to deter police misconduct, little would be gained when it could be shown that the police officer tried, but failed, to follow the stipulations of the law. The issue was ripe for judicial consideration.

The Supreme Court accepted for review two cases that asked the justices to consider instituting such an exception. *United States v. Leon* and

---

to sue for damages up to $25,000. Stewart, Lecture, April 28, 1983, p. 18.

23   Ibid., pp. 20-27.

24   Ronald Reagan, "Remarks at the Annual Meeting of the International Association of Chiefs of Police," September 28, 1981. Reported in *Compilation of Presidential Documents,* vol. 17 (Washington, D.C.: USGPO, 1981), p. 1041.

Massachusetts v. Sheppard both involved search and seizure violations, violations without malice and in fact an objective attempt by the police to follow the strictures of the Fourth Amendment. *Leon* arose when police officers innocently relied upon a search warrant that, through no fault of theirs, had been issued without probable cause. *Massachusetts v. Sheppard* also involved error but one that could hardly be blamed on the police. When a late afternoon search of the police precinct for the correct warrant form was unproductive, police used a similar warrant application. Indicating their problem to the issuing judge, the judge too made alterations to the search warrant and approved it. There was never any question that the police had probable cause to search. The only issue was a technical one, finding and using the correct warrant form. The search of Jimmy Sheppard, conducted with a warrant that at the time the police and magistrate both thought was lawfully enforceable, produced incontrovertible evidence that Sheppard had committed a brutal murder. It was only at trial that the warrant became contentious due to the slight of hand in altering the particular warrant form.

In both cases, the Supreme Court responded favorably (six to three) to the request for an exception to *Mapp* that would save from exclusion evidence obtained by officers who acted in good faith:

> As yet, we have not recognized any form of good faith exception to the Fourth Amendment exclusionary rule. But the balancing approach that has evolved during the years of experience with the rule provides strong support for the modification currently urged upon us. As we discuss below, our evaluation of the costs and benefits of suppressing reliable physical evidence seized by officers reasonably relying on a warrant issued by a detached and neutral magistrate leads to the conclusion that such evidence should be admissible in the prosecution's case-in-chief. We have frequently questioned whether the exclusionary rule can have any deterrent effect when the offending officers acted in the objectively reasonable belief that their conduct did not violate the Fourth Amendment. This is particularly true, we believe, when an officer acting with objective good faith has obtained a search warrant from a judge or magistrate and acted within its scope. In most such cases, there is no police illegality and thus nothing to deter. It is the magistrate's responsibility to determine whether the officer's allegations establish probable cause and, if so, to issue a warrant comporting

in form with the requirements of the Fourth Amendment. In the ordinary case, an officer cannot be expected to question the magistrate's probable-cause determination or his judgment that the form of the warrant is technically sufficient. "Once the warrant issues, there is literally nothing more the policeman can do in seeking to comply with the law." (*Stone v. Powell*, Burger, C. J., concurring). Penalizing the officer for the magistrate's error, rather than his own, cannot logically contribute to the deterrence of Fourth Amendment violations.[25]

Most of the legal community saw the inevitability of good faith. Nevertheless, *Leon-Sheppard* was front page news and the fodder for legal commentary and court critique.

By 1969 the Supreme Court of the United States had ruled that the *Lindway* case and the Ohio obscenity statute, initially at the heart of the *Mapp* controversy, were null and void. The vehicle for the legal change came in a Georgia case rather than in *Mapp v. Ohio*. In *Stanley v. Georgia*,[26] the justices unanimously ruled that the private possession of obscene material was not a basis for criminal prosecution. Here the police had entered the defendant's home in search of bookmaking paraphernalia, similar to the search for policy in Dollree Mapp's home. During the course of searching Robert Stanley's home, the police found an eight-millimeter film in a drawer in the bedroom, just as Delau and company had found obscene books and drawings in her bedroom. Stanley, like Mapp, had been arrested and charged with violating a state obscenity statute that criminalized mere possession. The effect of *Stanley v. Georgia* was to decide the *Mapp* case on its face, something that had troubled Justice Stewart eight years earlier.

For Carl Delau, the good faith exception was twenty-three years too late. Having searched Dollree Mapp's house with an affidavit, not with a search warrant as he assumed, his actions provided objective evidence of his good faith attempt to follow the law. Dolly had demanded the police obtain a

[25]   *U.S. v. Leon,* 468 U.S. 902 (1984) and *Massachusetts v. Sheppard*, 468 U. S. 104 (1984).
[26]   394 U.S. 561 (1969).

warrant. Delau complied, at least at the time he believed he had complied. *Mapp* in many ways is an earlier version of *Leon* and *Sheppard*. At the time the search was conducted, *all parties*—the police, the prosecutor, Mapp's attorney Walter Green, Carl Delau, and even Dollree Mapp—all believed that the search conducted by Delau, Haney, and Dever was under the auspices of a lawfully secured search warrant. The error by Lieutenant Tommy White, without malice, was one of inexperience, so this was hardly a case of deterrence. If the rationale for the Court in *Leon* and *Sheppard* was the lack of deterring police misconduct, the same could be said for the search in *Mapp v. Ohio*. Writing on July 9, 1984, in response to a *Cleveland Plain Dealer* article by James Neff on the *Leon* and *Sheppar*d cases, Delau said, "I feel I was justified in the action that we had taken on May 23, 1957 at 14705 Milverton Road and I feel much more justified and satisfied today."[27]

Carl Delau continued to rise through the ranks of the Cleveland Police Department. An officer with an impeccable reputation, his career was notable for his continued recognition. On July 9, 1962, Carl Delau was promoted to lieutenant. He worked in the fifth district in command of a uniform patrol and was later placed in charge of the Homicide Unit comprised of twenty-four detectives. By 1972, despite growing turmoil in the Cleveland Police Department (the new mayor, Carl Stokes, selected three different police chiefs over a two-year period), Carl Delau was promoted to the rank of captain. With a new mayor, new chief, and a new job, Delau was a crucial player in Cleveland law enforcement. Under his command were the Narcotics, Homicide, Robbery, Burglary, and Sex Crime Units. Later the Juvenile and Arson Units were also given to Delau. All told, the eleven units totaled 150 police officers including Mike Haney, now Lieutenant Mike Haney, in charge of the Sex Crime Units. Later, even though he resisted it, Delau was placed in charge of the citywide Vice Unit.

---

[27]   Letter by Carl Delau to James Neff in reference to the July 9, 1984, article by Neff, *Cleveland Plain Dealer,* July 10, 1984.

The mayor later disbanded the Vice Unit, returning the responsibility to district commanders. Captain Delau was placed in charge of the Special Investigation Unit with eight officers. Again with citywide reign, Delau was to address the numbers and gambling problem in Cleveland. Soon after, however, the Ohio Legislature created a state lottery, which greatly diminished the need for the numbers trade. Delau was in such a position now that his power was a commodity that politicians used as a bargaining chip. New mayors and chiefs made his future feel limited, and on March 31, 1978, Carl I. Delau retired from the Cleveland Police Department.

By the 1970s, politics was a main ingredient in curbing vice. After thirty-two years of service, Delau found himself at the center of the controversy rather than the catalyst of one. He was the story, not the crime that he had rooted out. Richard D. Hongisto, the police chief at the time, transferred Delau from vice to patrol captain for the far west side of Cleveland. As reported in the *Cleveland Plain Dealer*, Hongisto implied that Delau and the Vice Unit had questionable ethics. Delau was quoted as saying "I was treated wrongfully. I'm not happy. I think I can fairly say I'm the most knowledgeable policeman in vice, rackets and gambling, and I did more to curtail these than anyone else. Putting me back in uniform is like putting a football coach on parking lot duty."[28] Offended by the transfer, he resigned after serving five years as the chief of homicide, five as vice commander, twelve in the Vice Unit, and three as detective. Some of the most notorious criminals in Cleveland, a few well-known to readers here, Shondor Birns, Danny Greene, Donald King, and even Dollree Mapp had encountered the crime fighter. Hongisto was fired a week prior to Delau resigning.

Delau, in retirement, still is involved in police work. He works with Bluecoats Inc., an organization that he founded to assist widows and children of police and firemen killed while on duty. Delau was secretary of the Bluecoats from 1962 to 1978, serving as the liaison between the widows and

---

[28]   *Cleveland Plain Dealer* article. Date unknown. It was given to the author by Carl Delau.

the insurance companies. He often went and talked with the local bank president to give a thousand dollars toward funeral expenses. The group proved invaluable to the family when an officer died. He is an honorary member even today and still attends their events. He also keeps in contact with the Mounted Police Unit in Cleveland, the very group that he saw on parade as a young boy which encouraged him to enter public service. Recently the unit selected a woman to be in charge. Delau was delighted and commented to me that it was a needed change.

At eighty-four he shows little signs of slowing down or mellowing. He is active in the reunions of his old calvary unit and even returned to Europe fifty-five years after being there. He did not find any of the old foxholes but remembers fondly his time in the service and the friends he made. He even bought an M-1 rifle that is a must-see for the gun enthusiasts at the Beaver Creek Club, which he remains president.

Alas he is mortal!! A rotator cuff surgery left him with a more limited shooting schedule. This was the first surgery he had since World War II. On May 21, 2001, Carl Delau had several brief strokes and momentary speech loss. Surgery cleared some arteries and he had an ulcer removed from his carotid artery. He slowed down briefly, using the time to read up on World War II. He recovered quickly and is back in the swing of things, busy with his gun club, veterans associations, and dear friends such as Doris O'Donnell, who reported on his crime fighting for the *Cleveland Plain Dealer* for many years.

Time has not altered his opinions. Reflecting back to the events in 1957, Delau states he would react the same way today. He believes he did no wrong. The problem was the court, which created a rule that they later retreated from. In his mind, the real victim here was not Dollree Mapp but policing and policemen like himself. The exclusionary rule as an enforcement provision of the Fourth Amendment was aimed at strong-arm police, not intuitive police who are streetwise. The search conducted by Delau was, in effect, *Leon* and *Sheppard*. He had acted in good faith in trying to follow the law.

In spending time with Carl Delau it is reasonable to believe that he was caught in a time warp. He searched Mapp like he did everyone else. He did not treat her differently and she was not singled out. What was different was the Court, the climate of change on the bench for the issue, and the opportunity to create the change. Delau, in operating under the status quo, conducted his search of Mapp in 1957 like thousands of others. Based on the information Delau, Haney, and Dever had, they believed that Virgil Ogletree was in her home and he was somehow connected to the bombing of Donald King's home.

Of course our conversations always and eventually return to the search warrant itself. Why was White asked to get it? Why did Sergeant John Ungarvy, the police officer most familiar with search warrants, not complete the task? He was in charge of getting warrants and typically did so for Cooney. When Delau called Cooney from the Mapp scene, he told him he needed a warrant because Dolly demanded one. Cooney okayed the procurement of a warrant, and with Ungarvy not around, Cooney gave it to Tommy White to take care of it. White filled out the affidavit and took it to the judge, who signed it. However, White did not go back to the clerk's office with the documents. Herein lies the error. The typical procedure was that an affidavit was filled out and sworn to by the police. The judge would then decide if the warrant was supported with enough evidence, i.e., probable cause. If so, the warrant was granted by the judge and the officer then went to the clerk's office to get the actual warrant. Later after the warrant was executed, the police returned it to the clerk's office who then filed it. This was typical procedure. White did all but go to the clerk, hence when he arrived at Milverton Road, he had with him only the affidavit. The crucial last step, converting the affidavit, signed by the judge and the police into a viable warrant, had been overlooked.

When White brought the warrant out and handed it to Delau, Delau immediately went forward with a search and never even looked at it. Back at the Central Station, Delau opened up the paper to file it and saw that it was an affidavit supporting a search warrant not the warrant itself. Delau did not panic. He thought perhaps Tommy White had left the warrant in the clerk's office.

Delau and Haney went to Frank Hafee's office the next morning, and with the help of the clerk looked everywhere, thinking that the warrant had indeed been procured but White had picked up the wrong piece of paper that he brought to Milverton Road. They checked in all the files and did not find it. When confronted, White said he was confused and, eventually, sheepishly apologized. Finally, it seemed that White never got the warrant. The clerk even offered to backdate a warrant for Delau and Haney. "I'll write it and backdate it." "No thanks. Wouldn't be right." Delau knew then that a search warrant had not been secured but it was too late. When the police told prosecutor John T. Corrigan, his reaction was to proceed as if they had it. But it should be remembered that the warrant wasn't that important at this time; it was the pornography charges. So to Delau, Haney, Dever, White, and Corrigan, it was only a minor glitch because the focus was not on the search and seizure but on the felony charge of possession of pornography. According to Delau, Mapp never knew that at the time of the search, the paper he handed her authorizing their entrance was not a search warrant, but only an affidavit in support of one.

Dollree Mapp's possession problems no longer concerned obscene and lewd items, they now extended to drugs. By 1968 she had moved from Cleveland to New York City. Located at 95th and Madison, Mapp operated a used furniture store, Amsterdam Furniture. On November 2, 1970, Mapp was arrested in her St. Albans, Queens County, home. Police seized 50,000 envelopes of heroin and stolen property estimated at least $100,000. "The haul consisted of 10 television sets, 10 fur pieces, 5 electric typewriters, 11 portable radios, several sets of fine silverware, and an assortment of antiques, including clocks, vases and candelabra."[29] The police also found a 3.5 pure brick of heroin, scales for measuring, and quinine and lactose used in "cutting" heroin for street sale. Armed with a search warrant granted by Criminal Court judge Daniel S. Weiss, the raid of Mapp's home was the result of an investigation by the Narcotics Unit.

---

[29]   *Call and Post*, November 7, 1970, 1A.

Mapp had been under suspicion for trafficking narcotics before. The November raid took place while she was out on bail awaiting trial for possession of almost a million dollars (street value) of heroin.[30] Arrested along with her was Alan Lyons, described by the police as her "youthful apartment mate." Lyons, the manager of Mapp's furniture store, was considered to be the major player of the two and used the Amsterdam Furniture Store as a front for the drug operation.

On April 23, 1971, Dollree Mapp was convicted and sentenced to twenty years to life under a new and tougher sentencing statute enacted in 1969. She argued in court that the drugs, like the obscene material found on Milverton Road, were not hers. "It was a frame. I wouldn't be here if I wasn't black and I wasn't the Mapp in *Mapp v. Ohio*."[31] Her employee, Alan Lyons, was selling drugs unbeknownst to her, she said. On May 26, 1971, she was sentenced to prison by Judge Paul Balsam and began serving her time at the Bedford Hills Correctional Institution for Women at Bedford Hills, New York. She later appealed her conviction on the grounds that the search and seizure of evidence from her home violated her Fourth Amendment rights. Her claim was denied.[32]

Mapp's tale of her arrest, conviction, and sentence are much more colorful. She told of corrupt officers who not only seized drugs, but diamonds and coins. She claimed that she was targeted and arrested because she was the famous Mapp of *Mapp v. Ohio*. Despite regular harassment in prison, Mapp claimed she "had her clothes sent in from Neiman Marcus" and refused to eat prison food, claiming in all her time, she never did. Dramatically she recounted attempts by the warden to demean her and suggested sexual favors were required of all prisoners, even the high-profile inmates. Eventually Dollree was

---

[30]   Ibid.

[31]   "Six Defendants Whose Cases Changed American Law." *People Weekly*, May 5, 1975.

[32]   *Dollree Mapp and Alan Lyons v. Warden, New York State Correctional Institution for Women, Bedford Hills, New York and Warden, Great Meadow Correctional Facility, Comstock, New York*, 531 F.2d 1167, United States Court of Appeals for the Second Circuit, March 16, 1976.

paroled and her sentence commuted after serving nine years, four months, and seventeen days. Her send-off from the confines of Bedford Hills was recorded on several evening news stations and included a small crowd of well wishers.[33] Retelling these stories, Dollree Mapp paints herself as the victim of circumstances, one again wronged by the system. She tells these stories with vigor and with colorful language bordering on the vulgar, yet certainly at the same time reflecting an impressive sense of self. Fiction or not, one must admire her spirit and beguiling way in which she viewed the world. Even by the 1990s, when her physical appearance suggested a more humble and quiet soul, a sweatshirt-clad grandmother, her feisty rhetoric and personality revealed a persona more in keeping with her legal image. Her sense of spirit is admirable.

The fate of other participants in the saga of Mapp against Ohio are recounted here for those court aficionados and lovers of legal trivia. Jimmy Bivens, Dollree's previous husband, the father of Barbara Bivens, and the boxer who once fought Joe Louis, opened up a training gym for boxers on the west side of Cleveland in the mid-1970s. Retired from fighting since 1955, Bivens had a variety of occupations before coming back to boxing, this time to help up-and-coming young boxers. He was later found, in the mid-1980s, to be a virtual prisoner of neglectful relatives. He was found sick, penniless, and poor, locked in a dirty attic, almost dead from neglect. He was covered with bed sores and his own feces. He later recovered. Archie Moore, the former light heavyweight champion and Dolly's boyfriend, became a community relations specialist for the Boy Scouts of America and opened the ABC Club (Any Boy Can) in Cleveland with the mission of combating juvenile delinquency in inner-city youths.[34] Tom Dever, one of Delau's partners who engaged in the search of Mapp's home, died on the golf course in 1966 at the age of 43. Until his

---

[33]   Interview with Dollree Mapp, March 15, 1993.

[34]   Clipping file on Archie Moore, Cleveland Public Library. Includes articles from the *Call and Post,* May 3, 1963, and April 26, 1969, from the *Cleveland Plain Dealer,* April 22, 1969, and from the *New York Times,* February 12, 1969.

recent death, Mike Haney remained friends with his longstanding partner, Carl Delau. The two retired policemen would regularly chat and occasionally meet. Delau, the more gregarious and outgoing of the two, often instigated such encounters.[35] John T. Corrigan, the prosecutor, succumbed to the slow and tragic disease of Alzheimer's. Virgil Ogletree, the suspected bomber whose suspected presence was the reason the police came to Dollree's home in the first place, at eighty-one years old, was charged on August 12, 2003, for his involvement in a massive gambling network that operated an illegal lottery in Cleveland. Ogletree's gambling career has now spanned almost fifty years. He may never be tried, having recently been medically evaluated and diagnosed with Alzheimer's disease. Dollree Mapp remained friends with Virgil long after she moved to New York.

And then there is Don King. His rise from a local numbers gambler to boxing promoter and CEO of media powerhouse Kingworld is the stuff of rags to riches legends. Along the way he was convicted of second degree murder and sentenced to life in prison. Mysteriously, his sentence was reduced to manslaughter, and after serving less than four years, Don King was released. He later received a full pardon from Governor Rhodes. In 1976 he received the Urban Justice award alongside Justice William O. Douglas.[36] King became one of the most, if not the most, powerful promoters in sports. A quick glance at the Kingworld website provides a multimedia record of his successes. King now resides both in New York and at his boxing training facility in rural Ohio. His compound, complete with all the luxuries imaginable, includes his own golf

---

[35] One such encounter was arranged for my benefit. Carl Delau arranged for Mike Haney to pick me up at my hotel and drive me out to Delau's home in Novelty, Ohio. There Delau, along with Haney and Doris O'Donnell told stories of Cleveland in the 1950s and 1960s. The dynamics of the two men were fascinating. They were well matched as partners, each bringing a different set of strengths to the relationship. Their mutual affection and respect was the basis of a life-long friendship.

[36] Christopher Evans, "The Man Who Would Be King," *The Plain Dealer Magazine*, October 30, 1987, pp. 10-11.

course. "When I went from the numbers business to this business, it was just one promotion to another. One was live bullets, bombs and dynamite, and over here they just try to whup and kill you with words."[37] He is wealthy, well connected, and powerful.

---

[37]   Quoting Don King in Evans, "The Man Who Would Be King," p. 38.

CHAPTER TWELVE

Conclusion

> The exclusionary rule "developed like a roller coaster track constructed while the roller coaster sped along. Each new piece of track was attached hastily and imperfectly to the one before it, just in time to prevent the roller coaster from crashing, but without the opportunity to measure the curves and dips preceding it or to contemplate the twists and turns that inevitably lay ahead."—Justice Potter Stewart[1]

The road from good faith to the current Rehnquist Court is much the same as the path from *Mapp* to *Leon-Sheppard*. *Mapp* is still a quagmire, making the rule of exclusion both a blessing and a curse. It is a blessing because it curtails the actions of poorly trained, inexperienced, and negligent police officers. It yields no fruit for the brutal and harassing officer. Few of these exist (although of course, some do), with the majority of law enforcers being public servants who deserve the respect and trust of the citizens they protect. Herein lies the curse. The circuitous and litigious exclusionary rule has virtually created a non-rule. So fact-bound is the Fourth Amendment remedy that the predictive value of the exclusionary rule is almost nil.

If one cannot reasonably predict the outcome of a dispute over the interpretation of a rule of law, then it is a disservice to call it a rule. We can only expect the police to follow rules that they can understand. Currently the rule is so particularized it provides little meaning for the police to conduct

---

[1] Justice Potter Stewart in the Harlan Fiske Stone Lectures, April 1983, Columbia Law School. Quoted in "Congressmen Take Usual Potshots at Supreme Court Exclusionary Rule," *Chicago Tribune*, October 23, p. 1.

searches and seizures to gather evidence. Most well trained police officers abide by the rule as best they can. Tripping over the Fourth Amendment is easy for even the best of law enforcement professionals. To ask police to keep abreast of every Supreme Court decision interpreting the rule, about a dozen in any given year, is to ask them to be recreational law students as well as cops on the beat.

The broad brush of reasonableness, while lofty and principled, is meaningless in the face of practical real-life police-citizen encounters. This is not to say that the justices should write a bright-line rule but perhaps, instead, some rules that transcend the particulars of each case that comes before them. Such a step forward would serve all. It would protect the liberties of all citizens who might encounter a government agent with the discretionary power to enforce the laws of society upon them. It also protects the ability of those government agents to act with some assurance that reasonable behavior on their part is seen as reasonable. Both Carl Delau and Dollree Mapp would be well served by such developments. As it stands now, indeed as it did in 1957, the Fourth Amendment is tantamount to injustice for all.

The landscape of law enforcement, safety, and security is rapidly changing in the wake of the war on terrorism. Shortly after the attacks of September 11, 2001, Congress enacted the Patriot Act. Included in it are broader search powers, "sneak and peek" provisions, and relaxed provisions allowing high-tech surveillance and monitoring. If judicial interpretations of the Fourth Amendment are to be considered relevant to this public discussion, the judiciary must define police-citizen encounters in a way in which their application is useful and meaningful to both the police and the citizenry. While neither a bright-line rule nor a case-by-case approach have proved unworkable, perhaps there are tenets of fairness that express the concerns of James Madison as he wrote the amendment's text. A middle ground between all or nothing would make the Fourth Amendment something substantial.

✤ ILLUSTRATIONS

Fig. 1. The house on 14705 Milverton Road. Photograph taken by the author.

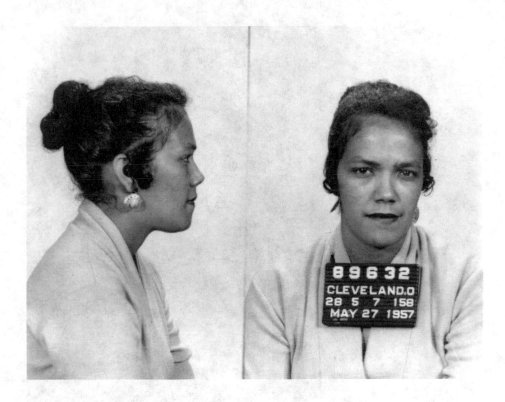

Fig. 2. Mug shot of Dollree Mapp taken after her arrest.
Courtesy of Cleveland Police Department.

Fig. 3. Captain Carl I. Delau, Cleveland Police Department. Provided to the author by Carl Delau. File photograph. Courtesy of the *Cleveland Plain Dealer*.

Fig. 4. Policy and clearinghouse paraphernalia including the dream book, policy balls and drawing and bet slips. Photograph taken by the author.

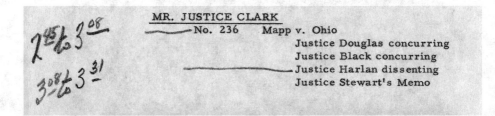

Fig. 5. Court Calendar, Monday June 19, 1961. Notations made by Chief Justice Earl Warren
indicating the time each decision, including *Mapp v. Ohio*, will be handed down.
Reproduced from "OT1960 (2) File," Box 145, Earl Warren Papers,
Library of Congress, Manuscript Room, Washington, D.C.

Fig. 6. Carl Delau with his beloved dogs. Courtesy of Carl Delau.

TEACHING TEXTS IN LAW AND POLITICS ⚖

David Schultz, *General Editor*

The new series Teaching Texts in Law and Politics is devoted to textbooks that explore the multidimensional and multidisciplinary areas of law and politics. Special emphasis will be given to textbooks written for the undergraduate classroom. Subject matters to be addressed in this series include, but will not be limited to: constitutional law; civil rights and liberties issues; law, race, gender, and gender orientation studies; law and ethics; women and the law; judicial behavior and decision-making; legal theory; comparative legal systems; criminal justice; courts and the political process; and other topics on the law and the political process that would be of interest to undergraduate curriculum and education. Submission of single-author and collaborative studies, as well as collections of essays are invited.

Authors wishing to have works considered for this series should contact:

> Peter Lang Publishing
> Acquisitions Department
> 275 Seventh Avenue, 28th floor
> New York, New York 10001

To order other books in this series, please contact our Customer Service Department at:

> 800-770-LANG (within the U.S.)
> (212) 647-7706 (outside the U.S.)
> (212) 647-7707 FAX

or browse online by series at:

> WWW.PETERLANGUSA.COM